DEC 2

THE ROBBER WHO SHOT HIMSELF IN THE FACE

AND 201 MORE STUPID BUT TRUE STORIES OF THE WORLD'S DUMBEST CRIMINALS

THE ROBBER WHO SHOT HIMSELF IN THE FACE

AND 201 MORE STUPID BUT TRUE STORIES OF THE WORLD'S DUMBEST CRIMINALS

GINI GRAHAM SCOTT

SPHINX® PUBLISHING
AN IMPRINT OF SOURCEBOOKS, INC.®
NAPERVILLE, ILLINOIS
www.SphinxLegal.com

Published by Sphinx Publishing, an imprint of Sourcebooks, Inc.
P.O. Box 4410, Naperville, Illinois 60567–4410
(630) 961–3900
Fax: (630) 961–2168
www.sourcebooks.com

Cataloging-in-Publication Data is on file with the publisher.

Printed and bound in the United States of America.
VP 10 9 8 7 6 5 4 3 2 1

AUTHOR'S NOTE

Where the stories come from published news accounts, I have used real names. Otherwise, in the interest of privacy, I have changed the names of the criminals. All the stories are real.

[CHAPTER 1]

UNBELIEVABLE EXPLANATIONS

Stupid criminals often get tripped up when they try to give unbelievable explanations for whatever it is they're doing. The following stories illustrate the wide range of such inane and insane explanations. Who would believe them? Judge for yourself.

A drunk was stopped for driving erratically. As the officer approached, suspecting another drunk driver, the man moved over into the passenger seat, and when the officer asked for his license and registration, he claimed he wasn't driving. It was the man in the back. But since the only "man in the back" was a big teddy bear, the officer quickly took the real driver in.

The driver of a GMC Yukon in Houston led the police on a twenty-five-mile, forty-minute chase, causing at least three wrecks along the way. He only stopped after jumping several curbs and flattening his front tire. He took off running and was tackled by a police officer. Why the long chase? The driver's excuse was that his parking brake got stuck and he couldn't stop. But the skeptical police soon discovered the real reason. The GMC Yukon was stolen, and the driver was on parole.

A police officer in Appleton, Wisconsin, stopped two men early one morning in the winter when he saw them walking out from behind a local restaurant that had been burglarized the night before. When he stopped them for questioning, he discovered they had a collection of likely burglary tools with them, including Channellock pliers, a screwdriver, and a flashlight. The men explained they were going to help a friend fix a toilet. But when the officer asked them the name of their friend, they couldn't give him a last name, phone number, or address. Then, the officer found a large crowbar stuck in a snow bank and the men's footprints in the snow, leading to the back doors of several businesses that had also been burglarized the night before.

Anthony Chiofalo, a twenty-two-year veteran police officer assigned to the Joint Terrorism Task Force, took a random drug test in 2005, and tested positive for marijuana. He was suspended without pay and subsequently fired, but tried to fight his suspension by arguing that his wife had spiked his meatballs with the illegal substance so he would fail his drug test and be forced to retire. The Police Commissioner refused to reinstate him, however, because the excuse was not credible.

In another case, a worker in Romania was accused of fraud and fired after he tried to get money from his company by claiming his mother had just died and he couldn't afford to pay for her funeral. Florin Radu Hretu, 27, from Pascani, Romania, asked his employer to lend him $300 to pay for his mother's funeral. His employer was very sympathetic and handed over the money. Unfortunately, luck was not on Hretu's side when a few minutes after his employer gave him the money, his mother turned up to pay him a visit—very much alive. Needless to say, he didn't get his job back—but he still has his mom.

A dentist in Woodland Hills, California, Dr. Mark Anderson, was threatened with losing his dental license after he was accused of fondling the breasts of twenty-seven female patients. He tried to argue that chest massages were an appropriate procedure in certain cases and even claimed that dental journals said that massaging pectoral muscles was a treatment for common jaw problems. Unfortunately for Dr. Anderson, he only used this treatment for his female patients.

In another case, a man convicted of being a serial flasher argued that he couldn't be guilty of the crime because his genitals were too small. The case occurred after Michael Carney, 41, of Fleetham Grove, England, was charged at the Teesside Crown Court with outraging public decency by flashing in front of six different women over a number of years. He argued that he couldn't have exposed himself because he was too embarrassed about the size of his penis to expose himself to women. He even showed the court explicit photographs taken by his wife that showed his smaller-than-average penis. However, he was soon convicted after the jury found out that he was earlier found guilty of sexually assaulting five women, and that on several occasions, he exposed himself to passersby while standing naked in front of his window. So, needless to say, whether he had small genitalia or not, the jury thought his small genitalia excuse was just a great big lie.

In a Florida case, the driver of a car that fled police tried to explain his decision to flee by claiming that he thought the package on his lap held a bomb, rather than the marijuana it actually contained. The case started when David Bennett was sitting in his car by the woods in Indian River County, Florida, at 2:00 a.m., when a sheriff's deputy drove by and thought he seemed suspicious. The deputy got out of his car and walked up next to Bennett and saw two bags

filled with marijuana sitting on his lap. Before he could make an arrest, Bennett stepped on the gas and took off, knocking down the policeman as he went. However, he didn't get far before he crashed his car. When the police officer followed Bennett to arrest him, the officer saw Bennett throw a bag of drugs into the woods.

Eventually, when the case went to trial, Bennett tried to explain away his actions by claiming that he thought the package in his vehicle held a bomb. He told the judge that he didn't know it was a police officer who was approaching his vehicle, and when the man pulled out a gun and threw a package into Bennett's car, he thought it was a bomb and just wanted to get away. Needless to say, the judge didn't believe him, especially with Bennett's fourteen prior felony convictions, and Bennett was sentenced to thirty years in prison. So you might say Bennett's unbelievable excuse really bombed.

CHAPTER 2

DUMB DISGUISES

Another reason that criminals screw up is that they use dumb disguises that look suspicious or that readily give them away.

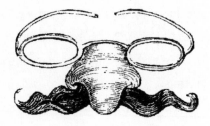

One robber tried to disguise himself before a bank robbery in Lafayette, Louisiana, by spraying himself with whipped cream. While it did completely cover his face, unfortunately for the robber, when he approached the bank teller to demand the money, the employees all began to laugh at him. Meanwhile, after the teller hit the silent alarm, and the robber waited to get his money, the whipped cream started to warm up, and slowly melted down his face. By the time the police arrived, the thief was easily recognizable, and he was easily arrested and taken to jail.

A duct-tape bandit didn't fare much better. Kasey Kazee, the would-be robber, walked into a liquor store in Ashland, Kentucky, wearing duct tape wrapped around his face to conceal his identity. As soon as he grabbed two rolls of change from the cash register, though, the store manager confronted him with a wooden club. Kazee tried to flee, but he didn't get very far. One of the store employees chased him out to the parking lot, tackled him, and held him in a choke hold until the police arrived.

Incredibly, after the police took him to jail, Kazee claimed that the police had the wrong man. Why? Because he said he had no memory of going into the liquor store or of the police removing the duct tape from his face. Unfortunately for him, the police had photographs showing him with the duct tape on him and the duct tape partially removed, showing his face.

A robber in Kenner, Louisiana, tried to use his shirt to conceal his identity. He stormed into a sandwich shop with his shirt pulled up over his face as his mask. The only problem was that before the robbery, he had been practicing pulling up his shirt to hide his face directly in front of the closed-circuit surveillance camera outside the store. He was easily identified and arrested.

Unbelievably, the same stupid criminal also robbed a motel down the street from the sandwich shop. In that instance, he entered the motel holding a towel with two eyeholes cut out if it, which he had intended to use as a mask to hide his identity. However, as he pointed his gun at the clerk and demanded money, he suddenly realized that his mask was around his shoulders. He had forgotten to put it over his face before he entered the motel lobby. In the middle of the robbery, he tried to pull the mask up over his face and line the holes up with his eyes. Of course, it was too late. The clerk had already seen him, and was able to identify him once the police arrested him.

Another would-be bank robber in Charlotte, North Carolina, simply didn't understand how to use his paper bag disguise properly. He started off with what seemed like a well-thought-out plan when he set off to rob the bank and took along his gun and a paper bag with eyeholes cut out. However, he decided to put on the mask several blocks from the bank while still driving. Several drivers wondered about the man driving around with a bag over his head and called the police. Then, when the robber went into the bank, still wearing the bag, and went up to a teller to demand money, the teller had a hard time understanding what he was saying, since he had neglected to cut a mouth hole in the bag. After some delay, the teller finally understood and handed over the money, whereupon

the robber ran out of the bank. However, as he exited, he was immediately arrested by the police who were waiting for him after being tipped off by the other drivers who had witnessed someone driving around with a bag on his head.

Even more bizarre is the bank robber who thought he could get away by disguising himself as a tree. It happened in Manchester, New Hampshire, when a man came into a bank one Saturday morning with tree branches taped to his body with duct tape. After patiently waiting in line with the other customers, he ordered the teller to fill a bag with cash, and then he fled the bank. Though he managed to get home and remove the branches from his person, he was soon arrested because his face could clearly be seen through the foliage on the bank's closed circuit television camera, which had recorded his every move. Needless to say, the media had a field day reporting the story, observing among other things that, "Police were not stumped by tree robber," that he "really went out on a limb in this robbery," and they hoped "he doesn't stick up any more banks."

nother bank robber in North Carolina thought he would be able to avoid someone using his clothing to identify him if he wore only his underwear. After walking into the bank in only his undies, collecting the cash, and running out, he was easily apprehended after someone called the police to report that there was a man wearing only underwear with strange bulges running down the street. Presumably when the police questioned him, they got the bare facts to help make their case.

One man broke into a funeral home in a small town near Valencia, Spain, and then tried to pretend to be a dead man when police and the business owner arrived. Unfortunately, his disguise didn't work for two reasons—first, he was the only corpse that was still breathing, and second, he was the only one wearing grungy clothing instead of the more formal attire people are usually buried in.

In Boston, two armed men—Jonathan Ortega, 23, and Miguel Angel Correa, 27—broke into a pizza parlor at a prearranged time, tied up the employees in the bathroom, and waited for a time-delayed safe to open, so they could steal the money. However, they decided to let one of the hostages go as long as he promised he wouldn't call the police. Of course, as soon as the hostage was released, he called the police, and they arrived shortly. Instead of turning themselves over to the police the two thieves tied themselves up and begged the pizza restaurant's employees to tell the police that the real thieves had already left and that they were all hostages. The employees didn't go along with the attempted disguise, and both men were arrested.

B ut as much as criminals might try to use disguises, sometimes no disguise will work at all, because the criminals are so easily identifiable. That's what happened when a thief shoplifted some shoes, socks, and boxer shorts from a small store in Cookstown, Northern Ireland. When someone saw him take the merchandise and described him to the police, the police immediately knew who the thief was because of his height—the man was seven feet, five inches tall and reportedly the tallest man in Ireland. In effect, he made a giant mistake thinking he could easily get away.

CHAPTER 3

FALSE IDENTITIES

Another ploy some criminals use is to attempt to create a false identity, so they can either get someone to do something they want or can escape being caught by pretending they are someone they are not.

One Milwaukee man who was arrested for impersonating an officer had decked out his car, a bright red 2005 Ford Crown Victoria, so it looked like an unmarked police car—with a blaring siren, flashing red and blue lights, a public address system, and bars on the rear windows. However, he made a mistake of driving by a real squad car while his siren wailed and his red and blue lights flashed.

When the real police officers called the dispatcher to find out if there were any emergency calls, and found out that there weren't, they followed the car and pulled the driver over. Inside the car, they found a nineteen-year-old male with an eighteen-year-old female passenger. The man was arrested and charged with impersonating a police officer.

Another man impersonating a police officer was caught trying to commit a crime in his Ford Explorer, which was rigged with lights and sirens. Harry V. Hackert, a fifty-year-old private security guard from Bucks County, Pennsylvania, ran a red light, activated his lights and sirens, and pulled over another vehicle. He approached the vehicle, waving around a loaded .38-caliber pistol and screaming at the occupants of the car. The only problem for Hackert, though, was that a real police officer was sitting in his real police car down the street, filming his every move.

Another man did a great job making his truck look just like a police vehicle, which he was using to help him impersonate a real police officer. Unfortunately for the man, he did not do as good a job making a fake badge as he did a fake police car. Instead, the man took a Chipotle restaurant gift card, blacked out most of what was on the card—leaving the Chipotle logo still showing—and scratched the word "Police" onto the card. He was caught after trying to pull a car over on the highway and showing this very fake-looking police badge as identification.

I n another cop car case, a man tried to play police-man to get home quickly after being trapped in commuter traffic. That's what happened in Tacoma, Washington, when a man in a late-model Ford Mustang decided that he had enough with the heavy traffic around four in the afternoon and flipped on his flashing blue front and rear lights and began zipping through traffic, occasionally turning on his speaker, which produced several tones that closely resembled the sounds of a siren on a police car. Unfortunately, the man never made it home, since another driver called 911 to report that a Mustang with flashing blue lights was heading north on the freeway and gave dispatchers a description of the car and its license plate number. Soon after, two State Patrol troopers in the area stopped the car, arrested the driver, and took him to the Pierce County Jail on suspicion of impersonating an officer. They also impounded his Mustang.

B ut perhaps the stupidest phony cop in a police car was the man who tried to pull over an off-duty police officer in Glendale, California, and was busted himself for his troubles. The bust began when Glendale Police Detective Keith Soboleski was driving on the freeway one night and saw flashing lights on the car behind him. Assuming it was an unmarked police car, he obligingly got off the freeway and pulled over. But he quickly became suspicious after the driver of the Honda Civic pulled up in front of his car, got out, showed him a gold-colored badge, said he was a cop, and told Soboleski he needed to slow down. In response, Soboleski asked the man to show him his photo identification and asked for a closer look at his badge. Suddenly, the fake cop became very nervous, turned, ran back to his car, and drove off. But before he did, Soboleski jotted down the license pate number and called in the case. The driver, Shadob Hosseini, was arrested the next day, standing right next to the car he used to pose as a police officer.

In another case, three teenagers dressed up as cops to have a chance to feel up women at the Munich Beer Festival. They singled out attractive women, and then—as they ran their hands over the women's bodies—pretended they were looking for hidden weapons. However, after some women complained about the unusually intimate searches, some real police officers caught the fake ones and charged them with sexual assault, indecency, and impersonating a police officer. You might call this a feel-good kind of case.

Then there was the john who posed as a police officer after a prostitute took his money and disappeared without delivering any services. The man, Ronald J. Auriemma, 38, picked up a woman near Tampa Bay, Florida, gave her $60, and then drove her to a motel to get a room for the two of them. After the woman went in and spoke to the motel clerk, though, she left. When she didn't return, Ronald decided to play cop. He went into the hotel and asked the clerk where the woman went, saying he was an undercover police officer conducting a sting and that the woman was wanted for theft and prostitution. The clerk asked to see his identification, and Ronald claimed not to have one because he was undercover. He was also unable to show a badge or a gun. Ronald wrote down his name and cell phone number so the clerk could call him if the woman returned to the motel.

After Ronald left, the clerk called the Port Richey police to verify if the story was true. The police sent

out a real police officer to investigate, and just as he arrived at the motel, Ronald appeared to see if the woman had returned. So not only did Ronald lose his money and not get what he had hoped for from the prostitute, but he got arrested for impersonating an officer as well.

In another case, a seventeen-year-old boy in Goochland, Virginia, tried to get his girlfriend out of summer school by pretending he was a plainclothes police officer. Apparently, his girlfriend wanted out of school for the day, so he appeared in the administrative office dressed in ordinary clothes, claiming to be "conducting a drug investigation," and said he needed to speak to a fourteen-year-old girl at the school about the case. But before he could spirit her away, the school officials called the Sheriff's Office about this so-called drug investigator from their office, and soon after deputies arrived and arrested him.

A thirty-four-year-old man from Los Angeles, Larry Lee Risser Jr., started inventing his own CIA identity when he was hanging out at a shooting range in Oxnard called Shooter's Paradise, and the tale he created gave him a colorful cachet. He claimed that he was the son of a U.S. ambassador and that he had made millions in the security business after exporting bulletproof cars to the Philippines. He also claimed to one person that he was Angelina Jolie's bodyguard for a time, and he told another that he was headed to Washington to receive the Silver Star. He even wore an official-looking badge on his belt to support his claim that he worked for the CIA, though when people asked to see his credentials, he told them these were strictly confidential.

But in January 2006, his lies began to unravel when he tried to con a friend, George Rice, who owned a gun shop next to the shooting range. He called Rice claiming he had been wounded in an ambush during a secret CIA assignment and that he needed $10,000 right away to get a rescue helicopter. Ever the friend, Rice transferred the money to Risser's account and later Risser told him he was recovering in Germany. But when Risser called Rice to send him more money, claiming this time he needed the money to escape from another failed mission, Rice got suspicious and called the authorities. Meanwhile, Risser's pleas for help seemed suspicious to the owner of the Shooter's Paradise, who initially was going to send him a check but then canceled it and contacted the authorities, too.

As a result of going too far with his CIA persona, Risser's scheme soon came to a crashing end, and instead of continuing to recover in Germany, he was back in Los Angeles facing federal charges for impersonating a CIA officer and wire fraud for conning Rice and another man out of $20,000.

One man posed as a priest to steal from a local grocery store. Brian Rush, 28, dressed in black, wore a white strip of cardboard around his neck, and a cross on his chest to play the part. He began going to a small grocery store in West Pittston, Pennsylvania, and asked the store clerk to charge his grocery purchases to the nearby St. Rocco's Roman Catholic Church, which already had an account set up at the store. Initially, the clerks obliged. However, Rush started to include nonnecessities among his other purchases, including energy drinks and cigarettes, which made the clerks suspicious. Next time Rush entered the grocery store to use the church's account, the police were waiting to arrest him.

Sheyrima Silvera advertised her services as a reverend on an online message board and offered to perform wedding services. One not-so-lucky couple hired her, and she conducted their beautiful wedding ceremony in their backyard. Silvera even filed the couple's marriage license, so the wedding was legal. However, after the wedding ceremony was over, Silvera took off with most of the gift cards that had been given to the couple, many of them meant to help the couple remodel their kitchen. The couple began to suspect that something was wrong when they received very few gifts after the wedding, even though almost one hundred people attended the wedding. However, they knew they had been robbed when guests started calling them over the next few weeks to ask what they had purchased with the gift cards. After the couple called the police, the investigators were able to trace the used cards back to Silvera, who claimed they were her tip for the service. The couple denied it, and Silvera was arrested. You might say she made the mistake of looking a gift card in the mouth.

In another case, two men posing as gardeners turned a Greek Orthodox nunnery into a marijuana plantation and led the nuns to believe they were simply growing decorative plants. The gardening enterprise began in the village of Filiro, near the northern port city of Thessaloniki in Greece, when two men arrived in town and told two elderly nuns at a convent that they would like to help them with their garden. It seemed like a charitable offering by two men who just wanted to help, so the nuns enthusiastically accepted their offer and the men planted over thirty marijuana plants there. As the plants grew larger, the nuns simply assumed they were decorative plants. However, the pot-growing scheme soon went bust when the police got an anonymous tip and raided the convent.

One fifteen-year old boy pretended to be a bus driver, and nearly got away with it, as he picked up and dropped off passengers along the regular route. In the Dutch town of Apeldoom, the fifteen-year-old stole a bus when the real bus driver stopped for a bathroom break. A few dozen passengers were already on the bus, but didn't notice anything wrong. The boy stopped from time to time to pick up passengers and drop others off at their destination, without anyone becoming suspicious that he looked especially young to be driving a bus. He probably would have gotten away with it, too, since all investigators had to go on was a bus and no complaints from passengers that anything was out of the ordinary. But then, he tried to do it again the next day, and this time officers were ready for him.

ot every criminal can effectively play the blushing bride, as one terrorist suspect discovered when soldiers at a checkpoint at Taji near Baghdad stopped what seemed like a wedding convoy. The soldiers asked all the cars to stop at the checkpoint for a quick search. However, one of the cars didn't stop until ordered to do so at gunpoint. Inside the car, the soldiers found some very nervous passengers including the only woman, a bride, in the entire convoy. They

found this extremely suspicious for a wedding party, which would normally have more female participants. Their suspicions were further aroused when the soldiers asked one of the men to lift the bride's veil and he refused.

And for good reason. When the soldiers ordered everyone out of the car and lifted the bride's veil, they found a stubbly-faced man, Haider al-Bahadi, instead of a blushing young bride. So instead of proceeding on to the wedding, the bride and his groom, Abbas al-Dobbi, were arrested on terrorism charges and sent off to jail, as were two other members of the wedding convoy who were also in the car.

CHAPTER 4

NOT KNOWING HOW THINGS WORK—OR USING THINGS THAT DON'T WORK

Sometimes criminals get tripped up because they don't understand some simple facts about cause and effect and technology. They either don't know how things work, or they have equipment that malfunctions. Either way, they can't do the crime properly and they get caught.

One man, trying to run away from the police after a drug buy, ran to a nearby railroad yard and grabbed onto the handrail of a train speeding by. But, instead of getting on the train as he expected from seeing daring escapes in the movies, the train knocked him down and dragged him ten feet down the track. When he tried to grab onto another car, the train knocked him unconscious.

A burglar trying to break into a building thought he could slide down the air vent, land on his feet, and steal whatever he could carry. Unfortunately, the shaft opened and dumped him down a nine-foot drop. As a result, he was pinioned with a broken leg over the weekend. After the police picked him up, he spent the next several weeks recuperating in the hospital.

A would-be thief thought he was being smart by taking the lens off a surveillance camera before he started to take anything. However, as he removed the lens, the video camera took a close-up shot of his face, while a camera across the room snapped a picture of him taking off the lens.

One gun-toting robber tried to hold up a store in Long Beach, California. When he pointed his .38-caliber revolver at the store owner and pulled the trigger, his gun failed to fire. So what did he do to figure out what went wrong? He peered down the barrel of the gun, and then pulled the trigger again. And this time it worked.

Another would-be robber walked into a small neighborhood grocery store, pulled out a large black handgun, and aimed it at the owner, a woman in her mid-sixties. Then, still waving his gun, he ushered her from the counter into the office area, where he demanded that she give him all the money that was in a small floor safe. Terrified, the woman complied and put the money into a paper sack. But then—perhaps showing off—the young man turned the gun barrel toward his face and pulled the trigger, which shot a stream of red cherry Kool-Aid from the barrel into his mouth. The woman, furious at being robbed by someone carrying only a squirt gun, picked up the bag full of rolled coins and began beating the young man senseless. Soon after, the police arrived and arrested the thief.

An undercover narcotics agent was trying to get to know a longtime suspected drug dealer, a man in his mid-thirties, who had been eluding the police for months. After a few weeks, the agent seemed to be gaining the man's confidence, and one night the two went to a bar together, where the dealer started bragging about his ability with a handgun. Suddenly he stood up, reached inside his jacket, and pulled out a semiautomatic pistol. Then, grinning, he pointed the gun at the cop's head, and for a few tense moments, the cop was sure he had been burned and was about to meet his fate, when the dealer just laughed and said, "I just bought this bad-boy, today. Been practicing my draw. Watch this." Then, he put the gun back in his holster, made a big show of breathing deeply and flexing his fingers, and quickly reached inside his jacket to demonstrate his skills. But when he grabbed his gun and fired, he shot himself through his own upper arm, hitting a vein. As the blood poured out, and he sat down on a stool in shock, he told the cop, "Man, I'll give you an eight-ball if you'll go call my mom." The officer was glad to make the call to the dealer's mother for him, but only after he first called the station to get a uniformed police officer over to the bar to arrest the man.

A robber walked into a bank in Merced, California, and went up to the teller. He pointed his bare finger at her—forgetting to put it in his pocket so she wouldn't see that it wasn't a real gun—and the teller asked the robber to wait, and she walked away. After a few minutes, though, the robber got tired of waiting and left the bank without any money. He might have gotten away with it, but instead he headed to another bank, where he jumped over the counter and tried to take the cash-drawer key from the teller by force. But he was unsuccessful when another employee grabbed the key and told him to go away. Shortly after, the police found him nearby sitting in a clump of shrubs and arrested him.

Two other robbers also ran into problems when they tried to break into a grocery store safe in Larch Barrens, Massachusetts, thinking they could use a laser they had stolen earlier that day from a local amusement center. They thought they would be able to cut an opening in the safe using the laser, just like they had seen in the movies. But, as they continued to shine the red beam at the safe without making a hole, they began to wonder what was wrong. Whatever they thought was wrong with their technique, they kept beaming the light at the safe until the police arrived and arrested them. Only then did the would-be burglars realize that they had stolen a battery-operated toy gun used for laser tag. They had simply been beaming a harmless red light at the safe for almost an hour. No wonder they couldn't burn a hole in the safe, though you might say they both had holes in their heads.

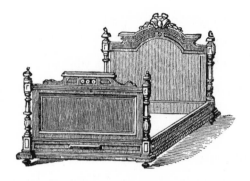

In another stupid and failed robbery attempt, a woman tried to hold up a Howard Johnson motel in Lake City, Florida, using a chain saw. Perhaps she was inspired by one of the chain saw horror movies that were popular at the time. However, the chain saw she brought with her was electric and she forgot to plug it in before the hold-up attempt. No one was hurt, and she was soon arrested. So you might say her attempt at robbery just didn't cut it.

In one case, a man trying to impress his girlfriend stole a plane that he couldn't fly. Michael Santos, 38, had too much to drink one Friday night and took his girlfriend to the local airport in LaPorte, Indiana, where he attempted to steal a plane. The two of them climbed into the cockpit of a twin-engine plane, and he began driving it down the taxiway. All of a sudden, flames began shooting out from the left engine. At once, he turned off all the switches, but as the engine continued to shoot flames and the plane continued to move, Santos missed the curve leading to the runway and plowed into a soybean field, where they finally got stuck.

Two thieves broke into the Fleetlink GPS Company in Queensland, Australia, and stole over $13,000 worth of GPS equipment, including a demonstration pack, a laptop computer, and a half-dozen in-car navigators used by transport companies to monitor their fleets. For some time, the police didn't have the slightest idea where the equipment was, though the company's business development manager, Murray Griffith, was hopeful that a thief would plug in the navigators, "because it looks like something to plug in." That's exactly what one of the thieves did five days after the heist. As a result, the software in the GPS system immediately let Fleetlink know exactly where the stolen equipment was. After the Fleetlink owners and employees had a good laugh about that, they contacted the police, who quickly busted the theft ring and recovered a huge stock of stolen equipment.

In a similar case in Lindenhurst, New York, three thieves stole fourteen global positioning system devices from a Town of Babylon Public Works garage, thinking that they were getting away with cell phones, which they planned to sell. The town immediately turned on its GPS-monitoring system, which showed that one of the devices was located inside a nearby house. When the police arrived at the home, one of the thieves was still holding the device in his hands.

CHAPTER 5

SLEEPING ON THE JOB

While most criminals flee the crime scene as soon as they can, some have gotten caught for falling asleep when they stay too long. As these stories show, if you want to commit a successful crime, don't fall asleep on the job.

One burglar decided to make himself at home in his victim's house, after he saw the owner packing her car for what looked like a long weekend trip. After she left, he broke in and scooped up her jewelry, cash, and other valuables into a pillowcase. But instead of leaving right away, he made himself at home, cooked up some food from the refrigerator, and fell asleep on her bed with a tray of food beside him while watching television. When the woman returned just a few hours later, her business trip having been canceled, she found the side door of her house broken open and called the police. They soon arrived and found the crook sound asleep.

Another sleepy burglar, Tiffany Casebolt, 24, made herself at home in the homeowner's bed in Huntington, West Virginia. Casebolt had already put some stolen items in her pockets and had several bags of other items nearby, ready for her to carry out with her. But instead of leaving, she settled in on the victim's bed, and when the homeowner returned home from work, he found his home burglarized and the burglar still asleep in his bed. He let her sleep until the police arrived, who then woke her up and took her to the jail.

A twenty-eight-year-old burglar in Traisen, Austria, similarly conked out after downing a bottle of vodka, and fell asleep in his victim's king-sized bed. When the homeowner returned home, he found the man, fully clothed, snoring away, with the empty vodka bottle beside him and the homeowner's wife's jewelry stuffed into his pockets. With the burglar still snoring, the homeowner quickly called the police, who arrested the man and charged him with breaking and entering.

Another burglar fell asleep under his victim's bed in Whitley Bay, England. In this case, the twenty-four-year-old burglar, Mark Smith, of North Shields, England, crept quietly past the homeowner while she was ironing, and she didn't hear a thing. Once upstairs, he took some gems from a jewelry box and helped himself to the woman's checkbook. But apparently, before breaking into the house, Smith had downed some vodka and Valium earlier that morning, so he was soon off to sleep. When the homeowner came upstairs, she found Smith's legs sticking out from under her bed. She even shouted and shook the burglar, but Smith was fast sleep. When the police officers arrived at the scene, they weren't able to wake him up either. Eventually, they were able to drag Smith, who was wearing a rucksack and clutching a pair of stolen gold earrings in his hand, from under the bed and off to jail.

In another case, a burglar in Burnley, Lancashire, England—Michael Arthur Bolton, 35—got sleepy after taking a tranquilizer and fell asleep on a settee before he could leave the house he had just broken into with the loot. The next morning when the homeowner heard noises coming from her living room at 6:00 a.m., she called the police rather than confront whoever made the noise herself. When the police arrived, they found the still-sleepy Bolton wearing one of Miss Robinson's jackets over his tracksuit, and in the bottom of the tracksuit, they found jewelry and sweets he had taken from the house. Outside the house, they found a bag filled with other items he had tried to steal from Miss Robinson.

imilarly, a tired burglar in Maglaj, Bosnia, was discovered fast asleep on a couch after he took a rest in a house he was burglarizing. After he broke in and stole two bracelets and an earring, he saw the couch, sat down to rest for a while, and fell sound asleep, where the homeowner found him when he came home. And that's where the police found him shortly after the homeowner called them—still snoozing on the couch.

In the state of Johor, Malaysia, two twenty-something burglars, who decided to have a snack after stealing some jewelry and other valuables from the house they broke into, fell asleep after raiding the fridge. The two crooks broke into the house while the homeowner was away, and they successfully scooped up the loot. But instead of quickly slipping away, decided that they were hungry and helped themselves to a free meal. After that, they decided to test their luck even more and took a nap on the couch, which is where they were found, still fast asleep, when the homeowner returned. She called the police, who arrived in time to wake up and arrest the two men.

One man even fell asleep on a comfy bed in a furniture shop window in Bulgaria, though apparently he hadn't intended to burglarize the store. Rather, the sleepy intruder, David Gibbons, 30, was an Irish tourist on holiday at the Bansko ski resort who lost his way after drinking with friends and couldn't find his hotel. But rather than checking into another hotel, he broke into the furniture store by forcing open the front door and settling down to sleep in one of the showroom beds, which is where a staff member found him the next morning. The store employee called the police, who arrived and arrested the man.

A nother would-be crook fell asleep while reading a book in a rare-coin shop, presumably because he wanted to figure out which coins in the display were worth the most. Apparently, the burglar was so overwhelmed by the vast variety of coins that he opened up a book describing their various grades. Perhaps because this made for dull reading, he drifted off to sleep. And that's where the police discovered him the next morning—fast asleep—with the book about coins open on his lap.

A robber attempted to hold up a local pizza parlor in Akron, Ohio. As he pointed the gun at an employee, the robber slipped on some grease that had been spilled on the floor earlier in the evening. He fell hard with a resounding bump on the floor and was knocked unconscious. He was out cold when the police arrived to arrest him and took him to the cooler.

Then there was the burglar who fell asleep in a bank in Cyprus, Turkey, after he broke in at night through a window and tried to break into the ATM machine. When he couldn't crack the code to open the ATM, instead of taking that as a good sign to leave, he feel asleep on the floor in front of the ATM. Unfortunately he didn't wake up in time to make an early morning getaway, because a janitor found him there two hours before opening time and called the police. As the burglar tried to sleepily stagger out of the building a few minutes later, the police were there to make the arrest.

Unfortunately, it doesn't make for a quick getaway when the crooks fall asleep in the getaway car, but that's what happened in Henderson, Tennessee, one fall night when six men decided to burglarize a home in the area. On the night of the planned crime, the men in the getaway car dropped four of the men off at the targeted home, and told them to wait in the bushes around the house for instructions. But the instructions never came as the four men waited in the dark, and when they finally got discouraged of waiting, they set off the home's burglar alarm as they emerged from the shrubbery. The police were quick to arrive and arrest the four men, and soon after, they found the other two burglars fast asleep in the getaway car, which they had parked in front of a nearby middle school. No wonder the men in the bushes never got any instructions— their accomplices were literally asleep at the wheel.

Another attempted robbery never got off the ground after one conspirator fell asleep, while the other ran out of gas. The two men hatched the plan after they were fired from their jobs at a car rental agency in Las Vegas, Nevada, and decided to rob the manager when he made his nightly deposit. Since they knew the time and the bank where he dropped off the money, they decided that one of them would wait for the manager with a gun, while the other would drive around the area to help the man with the gun get away.

On the night of the planned robbery, the driver dropped the gunman off at the bank about thirty minutes before the manager was expected to arrive to make his deposit. With plenty of time to spare, the gunman put on his ski mask and parked himself behind a dumpster where he could easily see the night depository. The plan went awry after he fell asleep behind the dumpster, so he never saw the manager make the deposit. Meanwhile, his partner drove around the block again and again at about three miles an hour until the car ran out of gas and he fled the scene on foot. The planned robbery never happened, although the next morning the police responded to a call about a man in a ski mask sleeping behind a dumpster, and nearby they found the car that had run out of gas.

An intoxicated thief who stole a car in Pretoria, South Africa, made the unfortunate choice of trying to hide in his car in a cemetery and falling asleep at the wheel. The thief stole the car from a nearby bar after a drinking binge. His biggest mistake was choosing a car with a vehicle recovery tracing system, so the cops very soon knew where he was. But the thief seemed to think he might be safe in the cemetery. Unfortunately for him, you can't hide very well in a cemetery. However, in this case, the intoxicated thief didn't even leave the stolen car to try to hide from the police. Instead, he simply fell asleep as the police discovered when they followed the tracing system right to the cemetery and woke him up to arrest him. So by trying to hide in a cemetery, you might say he didn't have a ghost of a chance to escape.

Finally, a nighttime burglar made the mistake of falling asleep in somebody else's car after he spent a long hard night burglarizing houses near Oslo, Norway. The forty-two-year-old burglar had already acquired a long list of criminal convictions, and after he was unable to stay awake on the job, he was on track to add another conviction to the list. After he collected his haul for the night, he tried to steal a car to carry home his ill-gotten gains, but he got sleepy, slumped against the wheel, and fell fast asleep. A passerby saw him hunched over the steering wheel and called the police. When the police arrived to check on the car and its slumbering driver, they found a familiar sleeping man in the front seat—who they knew from previous arrests—and the suspected stolen goods in the back seat. So once again, the sleepy burglar ended up in jail. As the operations leader for western Norway's police district, Harald Aase, had to say, if you want to commit a successful burglary, "You mustn't fall asleep on the job."

CHAPTER 6

EATING AT THE SCENE OF THE CRIME

Another big mistake some criminals make is eating on the go rather than waiting until after they have left the scene of the crime. As a result, some have literally been caught eating on the job.

One burglar, twenty-three-year-old Larcellus Angelo Scott, tried to order pizza after making himself at home in the house of his neighbor in Bakersfield, California, while she was out at work. Soon after he broke into the house, he phoned in a pizza order and began doing some laundry. While his wash was spinning away, he forged one of the woman's checks to pay for the pizza. But he never did get that pizza. Just as the pizza delivery person arrived, the homeowner also returned home from work and sent the driver away, telling him she hadn't ordered any pizza. The victim discovered Scott in her house when she opened her front door. Immediately he lunged at her, and she ran away to a neighbor's house, where she called the police. But did Scott leave? No. Apparently he was still waiting for his clothes to finish drying, and when the police arrived, they found him rummaging through the homeowner's purse, which she dropped when she fled. Needless to say, instead of getting any pizza and clean clothes, the burglar was treated to handcuffs and a ride to jail.

Scott Breyer, a twenty-something robber, forced himself into a home in Rutland, Vermont. Before going upstairs to steal things from the house, he fried himself up some eggs and made an egg sandwich. Meanwhile, as he puttered away in the kitchen, the homeowner heard him, called the police, and bolted herself in her bedroom. Before the police arrived, Breyer finished his breakfast and broke into the woman's bedroom through the bolted door, threatened her with a kitchen knife, and demanded her purse. She told him where it was, and he took it, cut her phone line, and left. But he didn't get very far, because the woman was able to provide an exact description to the police, and they found him close by, trying to hitch a ride.

Two men, broke and high on drugs after a night of partying, decided to rob a hamburger joint in Knox County, Tennessee. After driving to the first restaurant they could find, they piled out of their car with loaded shotguns and burst through the door demanding money and a dozen hamburgers with everything on them to go. A very scared employee told them that he would give them the money right away, but that they would have to wait ten minutes for the burgers because the grill was already shut down. One of the gunmen said they would wait. While they waited for their burgers, however, a passing motorist noticed the two men inside the hamburger joint holding shotguns and called the police. Just as the employee handed over the burgers, and the two men were about to head out, they heard police sirens and squealing tires outside. All they could think to do was to run, and in their panic, they left the money behind as they fled out the door. From there, they raced across the highway to the

river, where they scrambled down an embankment, hoping to hide under a bridge. But they weren't free for long, since the police came chasing after them with police dogs, who quickly found them—perhaps because the dogs could smell the robbers' greasy sacks of hamburgers. The dogs ate the hamburgers, and the police arrested the men. At least the dogs bit the hamburgers and not the crooks.

Nineteen-year-old Ruben Manzano became hungry after a night of drinking and decided he wanted a hamburger from a nearby Carl's Jr. in downtown Los Angeles. However, when he arrived, the restaurant was closed. Instead of finding a different restaurant, he simply broke in, turned on the grill, and started to fry up some burgers. But before he could finish cooking, he apparently got scared by something and took off running from the restaurant without his shirt and shoes. After a security guard saw him running down the street at 1:30 a.m., he called the police, who were able to find Manzano and arrest him on the suspicion of burglary.

CHAPTER 7

HOW NOT TO WRITE A WRONG

Some criminals get caught because of their writing—what they write or the writing they leave behind. Following are just some of the stories showing how stupid criminals have literally written their own ticket right to jail.

One liquor store robber quickly gave himself away after he entered a store in Pensacola, Florida, and decided to write a note to the cashier announcing a stick-up—because there were too many people in the store to do it out loud. He reached into his pocket for a piece of scratch paper and quickly wrote a note asking for money, which he gave to the cashier. For a few minutes, it seemed like he had pulled the perfect heist. The cashier read the note and quickly gave him all the money she had in her drawer. The robber quickly took the money and ran out the door, thinking he was home free.

But he had neglected to notice that he had written his note on the back of a letter sent to him by his probation officer—and that it had all of his contact information, including his name and address, printed on the front. Within a few minutes, the police were knocking on his door to announce that he was under arrest for the robbery. They had his note telling them exactly where to go.

Another bank robber in Englewood, Colorado, made a similar mistake. Forest Kelly Bissonette, 27, wrote his demand note on the back of his own personal check when he attempted to hold up the bank his account was in. He figured he would be smart by blacking out his name on the check so the authorities couldn't read it, but he didn't do it well enough. The police just had to hold his check up to the light to clearly see his contact information. Soon after Bissonette left the bank with about $5,000, FBI agents quickly tracked him down and arrested him.

ay stubs also don't work well for demand notes, as a robber in Delaware found. He walked into a convenience store, and after he handed the clerk his note, the clerk readily handed over the money. However, the criminal didn't have to wait long before the police arrived at his home to arrest him. They quickly located his name and address on the front side of the pay stub he had written his demand note on.

Another crook stupidly wrote a note on a piece of his own stationery, which included his full name and contact information. Carefully disguised for a bank robbery, he walked into the bank and handed the teller a note demanding several thousand dollars. He might have easily gotten away because his disguise was so good, but his personal stationary was all the authorities needed to track him down, reclaim the money he had taken, and put him in jail.

Barbara S. Joyner, 59, of Callahan, Florida, pulled into the drive-through lane of a local bank at around 3:00 p.m. in her yellow Nissan and demanded money from the teller. Her note stated that if she didn't get it, there were snipers all around and a person in the lobby who would set off an acid pack. After the teller turned over $34,000, Joyner sped off in her Nissan. However, since she didn't wear a disguise or hide her face, some of the bank staffers were able to identify her from a photo lineup. After a bit more research, the police discovered that her husband owned a Nissan Xterra. The police went to speak with her, and when they searched the family's vehicle, not only did they discover a notepad with markings similar to those on the note given to the teller, but they also found practice notes written on the same notepad. And then they found other robbery notes in different rooms in Joyner's house, as well as some money from the latest robbery in a bank wrapper. So you might say her involvement in the robbery was duly noted.

Mario Coleman of Memphis, Tennessee, thought he was being sly by acting like just another potential home buyer when he filled out an information card at an open house. But instead of making up a name, he signed his real one to the card. After waiting for an opportune moment to rob the real estate agent, he pointed a gun at her head and stole $25,000 worth of jewelry from her. However, within a few days the police had all they needed to collar Coleman. They took his name from the information card he had filled out at the open house, and put his photo in a six-person photo lineup, which they showed to the real estate agent. She quickly identified him, whereupon the police made an arrest and charged him with aggravated robbery.

An eighteen-year-old burglar who vandalized a building at a children's campsite by smashing crockery and releasing fire extinguishers was readily caught because he wrote his name on the wall, announcing that he had been there. With a black magic marker, in big letters, he wrote, "Peter Addison was here!" He also wrote the name of his gang—the Adlington Massiv—on the wall, too. All the police needed to do to find him and arrest him was to type his name into their computer system.

Craig C. Wilson from Henrietta, New York, traveled to Florida in a Mercury Mountaineer SUV. He left the car in a parking lot of a Jacksonville apartment complex, called GEICO insurance to report the car stolen and to make an insurance claim of more than $10,000, and flew back to New York. Six months later, his story fell apart after the owner of the Jacksonville apartment complex complained about finding the abandoned SUV in the parking lot. In the car, Wilson had left driving directions, which showed his route from his home in Henrietta to Jacksonville.

John Donovan of Cambridge, Massachusetts, a former MIT professor, entrepreneur, and multimillionaire, told police that he was shot by two strangers in the parking lot of his Cambridge office. He argued that the strangers were Russian hit men who were hired by family members. However, prosecutors claimed that Donovan wanted revenge after a legal battle with his children over the family fortune and had actually shot himself in an attempt to falsely frame his son. As evidence, the prosecutor said the police found a to-do list in the front pocket of Donovan's sports jacket when he was arrested. The to-do list appeared to outline how Donovan staged the shooting. This evidence was all the judge needed to side with the prosecutor and to sentence Donovan to probation and community service.

Leaving behind a gas station receipt in a stolen truck was not a good idea for a thief in Westlake, Ohio. He began by stealing a pickup truck in Sheffield Lake and then abandoned it in Westlake. Once in Westlake, he stole a different vehicle, which was later found abandoned in Sheffield Lake. Perhaps the thief wanted to commute back and forth and thought he might avoid capture if he drove two different stolen cars. However, the Westlake police soon searched the vehicle and found a gas station receipt in the truck from a Sheffield Lake gas station. They checked the still photos taken on the speedway between the two towns, and were able to get a clear photo of the thief, driving the truck and wearing a comic book villain T-shirt.

One of the most stupid things a bank robber can leave behind, though, is a resume and photograph of himself. Etni Ortiz robbed a bank in Tampa, Florida, but dropped his resume and some photos he happened to be carrying when the dye-pack exploded, leaving permanent red dye all over his money, resume, and photos. Nine days later, Ortiz attempted to rob a second bank in Sarasota, Florida, and gave the teller a note that read, "This is a robbery. Do not do anything stupid or I'll shoot you first. Give me all $100, $50, $20. No smoke bombs or I will shoot you." Ortiz fled with $1,860 the teller gave him, but he wasn't gone for long. The police used surveillance videos to determine that Ortiz had robbed both banks and issued an alert. The next day, a Florida Highway Patrol officer discovered Ortiz driving an SUV that he had stolen in Massachusetts. Inside the vehicle, the police found all the evidence they needed to tie Ortiz to both Florida bank robberies—a cap he wore in the

second robbery, which could be seen in surveillance photos, paperwork stained with red dye stuffed under the rear passenger seat, the note he had used with the teller, and a suitcase packed with $1969 in cash. With that kind of evidence, Ortiz pleaded guilty to two counts of bank robbery and one count of transporting a stolen vehicle, and he was subsequently was sent to jail. You might say the resume and note he left behind, along with the colorful paperwork and cash, helped to get him his prison job.

Eighteen-year-old Michael Alfinez posted a video online of his eighty-five-year-old grandmother—who suffered from dementia—wearing a ski mask, holding a gun, and making profanity-laden threats at the camera. After prosecutors saw the online video, Alfinez was charged with elder abuse.

Larry Black, 21, dropped a probation appointment card at the scene of one burglary he committed. Even more helpfully, he left his fingerprints on the card. Police had no trouble tracking him down and tying him to the burglary with that type of evidence. He probably didn't make his probation office appointment either.

Six days after he was released from police custody for burglary, seventeen-year-old Keirron Neal broke into a house in Rugby, England, and stole a treasured family recording of the daughter's first two months. He might have gotten away with it if he hadn't dropped a Warwickshire Youth Offending Card with his name on it at the scene.

Peter Matthew Tilloston, 22, broke into a store in Gillette, Wyoming, and stole three handguns, three shotguns, and a safe containing $12,000 in cash and $1,500 worth of jewelry. But before he could enjoy the fruits of his burglary, the police found his receipt for new tires for his truck that he had dropped at the scene—containing his name, address, and a description of his vehicle—which led them straight to Tilloston. Before he had a chance to spend the money or fence most of the guns and jewelry, the police were at his door to arrest him.

John Beckwith, a twenty-eight-year-old heroin addict, broke into a house one afternoon in northern England. After being evicted from his own home and living on the street with no money and nowhere to go, he first knocked on the door. After getting no answer, he crept through an open window, leaving an imprint of his sneaker on the windowsill. Thinking no one was there, he grabbed the house and car keys, bottles of alcohol, cigarettes, and a handbag containing credit cards and books, but then had a sudden shock when he walked into the homeowner's bedroom and saw her sitting on her bed having a cup a tea. She simply hadn't heard him when he knocked. At once, Beckwith fled from the house with his small haul of items, but unfortunately in his haste, he dropped a prescription bottle with his name on it, and the police were able to track him down and arrest him two days later.

A robber from Klamath Falls, Oregon, made the mistake of leaving his pants behind with his wallet and photo ID. Presumably the robber thought he was playing it smart when he took off his pants and shirt in a homeowner's front yard, before entering the house to rob it, thinking that the people inside would have a harder time identifying him later. He then broke into the house, knocked the victim to the floor, stole several items, and fled in his underwear. But in making his hasty flight, he forgot to take the pants, and his ID led the police right to him.

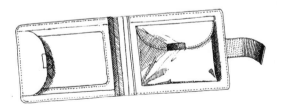

Another young man approached a counter in a grocery store in South Carolina with a shotgun and demanded all the cash in the register. After the cashier handed it over to the robber, the robber noticed a bottle of single-malt Scotch on the shelf behind the counter, and, waving his shotgun at the clerk, ordered him to add the bottle of Scotch to his bag with the cash. But the cashier refused, telling the man that he didn't think the man was old enough to drink. Though the robber said he was, the clerk still refused, so the robber pulled out his driver's license to show that he really was over twenty-one, and the clerk handed over the bottle. The robber left the grocery store thinking he had gotten away with it. The cashier called the police and gave them the robber's name and address that had been printed on the license, and the police soon made the arrest.

Three men broke into an unlocked Dodge Charger in Fort Lauderdale, Florida. However, the men couldn't find anything they wanted to steal, so they tried to leave the scene. Before they could all get away, a police officer arrived and was able to stop two of the men. The third thief kept running, but, unfortunately for him, in his haste he left his ID in the car. Police met him at his house when he returned home and arrested him.

L eaving an ID card in an apartment burglary is similarly a fast pass to prison. An ex-convict, forty-three-year-old Robert Alan Fry of Rock Island, Illinois, used his Department of Corrections identification card to jimmy the lock of an apartment, where he stole a plastic jug filled with about $400 in change. His goal was to buy some drugs and return to his motel room to get high. However, he left his Corrections ID behind, and the police easily found him the next day at the nearby motel. They arrested him and charged him with burglary, possession of drug paraphernalia, and interference with an investigation, and returned him to prison.

CHAPTER 8

LEAVING A TRAIL
OF EVIDENCE

Sometimes crooks leave a trail of obvious evidence, besides the left-behind writings and identification cards described in the previous chapter. Whatever they leave—and sometimes the leftovers are amazing—it makes it much easier for the police to find them.

Two women accused of shoplifting from a department store in Harsdale, New York, left one of their babies behind when they fled from the store. Even worse, the authorities found vases, teapots, and knives valued at $180 hidden under the covers of the stroller, right next to the purse and cell phone of the mother, Suzette Gruber. Soon afterward, the police were able to track down the child's mother from the information she had left behind. They also discovered that Gruber had previously been charged with several misdemeanors—petty larceny for stealing $272 worth of clothes and endangering the welfare of a child, since she brought along her fourteen-year-old daughter and two-week-old son the last time she was arrested.

A homeowner from West Bend, Wisconsin, returned home in the middle of the night to find a light on in his basement. He entered the house, and the intruder, interrupted while robbing the house, fled into the garage, unable to find his way out. When the burglar ran back into the house, the homeowner confronted him and pinned him against the wall. However, with a few twists and turns, the burglar was able to slither out of his pants and shoes, and ran off, wearing only a hooded sweatshirt and red boxer shorts. Meanwhile, hearing the noise downstairs, the homeowner's wife called the police. When they arrived, not only did the police find property in the burglar's pants they believed was taken from a car in the neighborhood, but they found the burglar himself hiding in the tall grass of a nearby wooded area. And naturally, since he wasn't wearing any pants or shoes, he was easy to identify.

Nineteen-year-old Jonathan Parker of Nashville, Tennessee, found several leather jackets irresistible when he was shopping at a trendy clothing store. When he found the prices a little high, he decided to be cagey and went into a dressing room, where he removed the magnetic strips. This way,

he figured, he wouldn't be detected by the store's sensor alarms in front of the exit. He carefully searched through the sleeves, pockets, collars, and waistbands until he was sure he had removed every strip. However, when he confidently walked to the front door, the jackets stuffed under his own coat, the alarm went off and a security guard immediately stopped and searched him. Although the guard couldn't find any magnetic strips on the jackets, he found several of them on the soles of Jonathan's shoes. After Jonathan had thrown them on the floor, he unthinkingly stepped on them, and the sticky strips did the rest. He was quite clearly stuck, exposed by the little magnetic strips he had tried to throw away, and the police easily arrested him and charged him with shoplifting—a charge that was likely to stick.

In another case, a burglar the police dubbed the "Cinderella burglar" left a tennis shoe behind when he scrambled out through a small window to escape from a house in Staffordshire, England. He fled quickly when the occupants of the house caught him trying to burglarize their house shortly after 6:00 p.m. But, like Cinderella, he left his shoe behind. The police were confident that they would soon arrest him from the victims' description of the burglar as a balding white man in his late twenties, and by his single shoe, since he would have to make his way home wearing either one shoe or none at all. Armed with that information, the police put out to the public—look for a young balding man wearing one or no shoes. You might call it a case of a shoo-in.

A pair of burglars broke into a grocery store in Dayton, Tennessee, at about 3:30 a.m., thinking they could pick up some easy cash. They used a concrete block to break in through the glass front door, and though they didn't find any money, they fled with twenty cartons of cigarettes worth about $650. And that proved their undoing. When two patrolman stopped at the store that night after a neighbor reported hearing its burglar alarm, they didn't find anyone at the store. Later that morning, another officer patrolling the area found several boxes of cigarettes on the ground near Cedar Glen Lane just up the road from the store. When that officer and another patrolman began talking to residents of the mobile home park there, they found a witness who saw two men running toward some apartments on Cedar Glen Lane during the night. When the officers went to the apartments, the occupants gave them permission to search. Big mistake. The officers found all the missing cartons of cigarettes and quickly arrested the two crooks. The trail of cigarette boxes had led right to their door.

A teenager in Belmont, New Hampshire, robbed the local convenience store, and then fled with his pockets full of change. However, he didn't realize that he had holes in both his pockets. So as he ran off, a trail of quarters and dimes fell to the ground, and the police just had to follow the money trail to his door.

In another case, from Green Bay, Wisconsin, a burglar who broke into a barbershop and stole a television on Super Bowl Sunday made the mistake of leaving his footprints in the snow. So it was very easy for the police to simply follow his tracks behind the shop to a nearby apartment complex. After following the footprints to his door, they found the criminal on his couch watching the Packers game on the stolen television. Too bad for him they asked him to pack it in before the end of the game and took him to jail.

In another case that was wrapped up quickly, three boys and a girl, ages fifteen and sixteen, broke into a gas station in Pasadena, Maryland, and stole some candy, chips, and cigars. But as they walked along the road, they left a trail of candy bar wrappers behind them, and a police dog located them about a quarter of a mile away. The police arrested them for burglary and theft.

Another robber made a fateful mistake when he left his car keys on the counter of the store he held up. He expected to do a quick stop and rob at a convenience store, driving up to the door, grabbing the cash, and then speeding away. Well, he got the first part of that right, and he successfully ran out with a bag full of cash. But when he got to his car, he realized he had left the keys behind. When he returned to the store to pick up his keys, the police picked him up instead, and he was promptly arrested.

L eaving drugs behind in a rental car is also not a good idea, as three drug dealers found after they tried to smuggle 135 grams of heroin into Germany from the Netherlands. Though the drugs were worth about $75,000, they left them behind in a first-aid kit where they had hidden it—too well, apparently. When the cleaners were getting the car ready after the rental company decided to sell it, they found the stash. Not only did the drug dealers lose their drugs, but they were also arrested and placed into custody after the police used the firm's computer records to track down the dealers.

One burglar made the mistake of leaving a trail of cornflakes behind that led right to her hotel room. That's what happened after thirty-one-year-old Amber McCarthy grabbed some cash from a florist's shop, along with a handful of flowers, and then accidentally scattered some cereal she had taken from the hotel where she was staying. The result was that she created a three hundred-yard trail of cornflakes as she returned to her hotel room. After the police followed her there, they found the cash and flowers she had taken. Then she not only admitted to that burglary, but to three others as well.

In another case, it was a fifteen-mile trail of doughnuts that fell out of a delivery truck that led right to the thieves. That's what happened when two thieves stole a Krispy Kreme truck from a parking lot in Slidell, Louisiana. The truck had been parked at a convenience store with its rear door open and engine running, while a deliveryman carried the doughnuts inside. The opportunity seemed too good to pass up, so the two thieves jumped in the truck and sped off to the nearby town of Lacombe. But they forgot to shut the door of the truck, and the doughnuts spilled out along the way. The police were soon on their trail, after hearing reports of "a dangerous driver who was losing his doughnuts." Though the men abandoned the truck and fled once the police spotted them, the police were able to capture the thirty-one-year-old passenger, Rose Houk, who explained that they had been smoking crack cocaine for several hours before they commandeered the truck. So why take the truck? "I don't know if it was a need for transportation or if they just had the munchies," police spokesman Rob Callahan commented. Whatever their reason, they sure ended up in a hole because of the doughnuts.

Food stains can also be a giveaway, as a German hit-and-run driver discovered after he caused an accident while eating some spaghetti with sauce. The accident occurred after twenty-eight-year-old Jens Martin stopped for a takeout meal, and then ploughed into two other parked cars while enjoying some spaghetti carbonara in the town of Goerwihl in southeast Germany. He figured he could make a fast getaway, and when the police turned up at his house, presumably because someone reported his license number, he tried to claim his car had been stolen. But his claim didn't hold up, since the police found the spaghetti stains still on his unwashed shirt, and they called it a match with the takeout spaghetti he had just bought.

E ating on the job can serve to pin a burglary on a crook, too, when the crook leaves some of the half-eaten food behind. That's what happened to a suspected serial thief in the city of Darmstadt, Germany, when he left a half-eaten slice of salami at the crime scene, and the police were able to extract a sliver of his DNA from the slice. In this case, the thirty-seven-year-old Romanian man was suspected of breaking into a workshop office, where he stole some cash and two locks and caused about $3,500 worth of damages. Apparently, he found the salami lying around in the office and just thought he'd have a bite. If it weren't for the salami, he might have gotten away with the burglary. But during a routine police road check, the German police arrested the man, who was already wanted in connection with nineteen other burglaries, and they discovered the DNA connection with the salami, tying him to the workshop break-in.

Jack Wright, a petty thief, broke into homes during the day in Sunnyvale, California, always picking a time when the owner was at work, so it was an easy in-and-out kind of operation. And his modus operandi was jimmying the lock on the back door using a credit card. Then he would quickly pick up a few items and just as quickly speed away before anyone saw him. But one time he made the mistake of leaving his own Sears credit card behind—and it was a quick and easy operation to identify him and pick him up.

In another case, from New Britain, Pennsylvania, Abdullah Muhammad made the mistake of dropping his wallet and leaving it behind after he grabbed some cash from the register of a convenience store. Muhammad probably thought that the best way to get the clerk to open the cash register was for him to make a purchase. When the clerk opened the drawer to take his payment, Muhammad made his move. He shoved the clerk aside and grabbed the money out of the drawer. However, he still had his own money in his hand, and when he grabbed the cash from the drawer, he dropped his wallet on the floor. Instead of stopping to pick it up, he ran. So when the cops came, all they had to do was look through his wallet and find his ID, which was all they needed to find Muhammad and make a quick arrest.

CHAPTER 9

PRINT IT

All kinds of left-behind prints—from fingerprints to footprints—are also a dead giveaway. And some criminals have even left behind their fingers, which makes them even easier to find. The use of prints to positively identify criminals has been around for so long—and dramatized so often on popular television shows—that you'd think that criminals would know this by now, but these stories prove that they don't.

Thirty-one-year-old Victoriano Vasquez nearly got away with a home burglary in Austin, Texas, when he filled some pillowcases with a huge collection of movies, some money, and other small possessions. Though he tried to steal a DVD player and some other electronics equipment, the homeowner arrived home unexpectedly after taking her three-year-old son to preschool, and the thief fled. Vasquez got away, but not for long. In his haste to steal whatever money he could get a hold of, he smashed the three-year-old's piggy bank. While he only walked away with $40, he left behind a perfect fingerprint on the bank—the only fingerprint he left behind. His fingerprints were already in the system for four past burglaries, and he was quickly identified and arrested.

One drunk man fled after being part of a large bar brawl in Sydney, Australia. He left the pub, not realizing that part of his finger was missing, and only discovered it after he saw a lot of blood on his hands and went to the hospital. The pub's security guard found the missing finger in a pool of blood in the pub, which proved to police that he had been part of the fight.

In another case, a burglar left part of his fingertip behind after he broke into a visitor center at Shelby Farms, a park outside of Memphis, Tennessee. He broke a lock, rummaged through an office, looked through the office manager's desk, and finally ran off with $400 in Honeybaked Ham gift certificates. But he didn't exactly make a clean getaway. Police found his fingertip on the floor, which was probably sliced off when he broke the glass door to get into the building, and were able to get a partial print from it.

Another burglar had the misfortune of losing part of his finger on a wire when he climbed into a builder's yard one night. The incident happened in Hampshire, England, when the thief climbed over the razor wire fence outside the yard to siphon some diesel from the gas tank, located just beyond the fence. Apparently he either didn't see or simply ignored the signs saying, "Beware of the razor wire." The wire took a deep slice out of the burglar, leaving his fingertip in a pool of blood. You might say the thief got fingered by the fickle finger of fate.

Josh Kirby, 31, from Framingham, Massachusetts, was accused of spray-painting graffiti on several businesses after the police caught him with blue hands. The police arrived after witnesses called to report that they saw a man spray-painting an anti–Ku Klux Klan message on the side of the Standard Electric building downtown. When the police confronted he denied any wrongdoing, but his hands were covered in blue spray paint, so they quickly arrested him.

Julius Jacob Ludwig, 36, and another man attempted to rob a restaurant in Bend, Oregon, by forcing open a window to get in one snowy night. An employee was already in the building and heard the suspects break in, so he called 911, and Ludwig and his accomplice fled before the police arrived. However, the police were led right to them by the fresh footprints they left in the snow, and easily arrested the men.

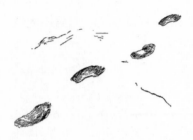

In a similar story from northeast Pennsylvania, Sean Donohue, 18, broke into a house. Unfortunately for him, it had just snowed, and police were able to follow his fresh tracks right to his parked car, where he was found and arrested.

The snow also helped the police in Juneau, Alaska, track down two suspects who burglarized and vandalized a school, causing over $7,000 in damage. It happened at the Dzantik'I Heeni Middle School, when the police saw an outside door and window broken shortly after 6:00 a.m., and discovered that vandals repeatedly threw large rocks, which damaged a stained glass window inside the school. But with a little help from Mother Nature, the police were soon on their way to the suspects by following a trail in the snow straight to the suspects' residence.

CHAPTER 10

NO TECH

While many criminals today are embracing the latest technology—from cell phones to computers—sometimes the very technology they use to help them commit the crime or conceal it is what gives them away. Following a series of screw-ups from criminals who literally turned high-tech into no tech because they didn't know what they were doing.

Two robbers broke into a store in Mesa, Arizona. At the time, the store was barely occupied, and as one robber distracted the employees, the other one grabbed a pair of wristwatches. Then, confident at the success of their first heist, one of the crooks came back the next day, and pulled a watch out of display case that the store owner was still repairing after the theft the previous day. Then, the thief fled to a waiting van, with the store owner in pursuit, and though the thief escaped into the van and drove away, Guertin manage to write down the license plate number.

The crooks might have gotten away with it, but the store owner had security cameras installed, which clearly showed the two robbers. He posted the video to YouTube, offering a $1,000 reward for information leading to the burglars' capture, and he handed the license plate number over to police.

In another case, a thief on the west coast of New Zealand, was caught after he was spotted on a video posted on YouTube. The thief, fifty-year-old Dawson Anthony Bliss, gained his claim to fame when the video camera taped him circling the store, stealing a laptop computer, slipping the computer into his overcoat, and leaving the store. Then, the store owner got creative and he posted the thief's performance, set to a music track from *The Pink Panther*, on YouTube, which soon became a featured video around the globe. It tracked over 500,000 hits, and one alert viewer recognized the thief and called the police. Soon after that Bliss was arrested, pled guilty, and was fined $1,485, plus ordered to pay about $1,500 in reparations by the judge.

Two other burglars ironically got caught on video tape in a store in Dallas, Texas, which sells high-end security equipment, and was naturally set up to provide its own camera security. In fact, the store—aptly called Spy Supply—had seventeen cameras set up around the store, and there were multiple warning signs posted all over the store telling patrons they were being filmed on camera. But the two burglars struck anyway. They broke in through the store's front door with a crowbar and then helped themselves to nearly $10,000 worth of spy equipment which they dumped into a trash can. Then, they fled with that to their getaway car, put it in, and roared away. And everything was captured on video, including a clear shot of their car driving away.

When he set up a video camera in a women's restroom at a movie theater the twenty-year-old Seattle man thought he would be in for a treat. But instead, he got the treatment when he was booked into the Kings County Jail on suspicion of voyeurism, after a twenty-four-year-old women spotted the camera in her stall and tearfully reported the camera to police. Then, when the police watched the tape, they saw not only her and three other women using the toilet, but the beginning of the tape caught a shot of the theater employee setting up the camera. After the police read him his rights, the man admitted taping the women in the theater, and he was arrested. You might even call it a photo finish.

In another case, a man's butt on tape provided all the identification police needed to make an arrest, The incident happened at a shop in Kentish Town in the United Kingdom, when Aaron Williams and an unidentified accomplice presented themselves to the clerk at the counter wearing masks. Williams pulled out a knife, demanded money, and fled the store after the clerk handed some over. The two criminals might have probably gotten away—since the investigating detectives found no fingerprints or DNA, and there were no eyewitnesses able to identify the robbers. But, when Williams bent over the counter to attack the clerk with his knife, the video surveillance camera clearly showed the buttocks of the heavily built Williams, which was somehow enough for the police to identify and arrest him.

One man literally got caught with his pants down when he took some nude photos of his stepdaughter when she slept. The man—forty-six-year-old Douglas Hanley of Manchester, Connecticut—was caught when his wife found the photos in one of his pants pockets while she was doing the laundry. And not only did the photos show the sleeping daughter, but they showed Hanley's hand in the frame pulling the girl's undergarments aside. His own photographs led him to being charged with voyeurism for taking the photos of the girl while she slept.

Students who posted photos of a planned attack on their school on MySpace were similarly exposed by their own photography. In this case, three high school students—Patrick Quigley, 16; Joseph Said, 16; and another unnamed student who was only fifteen—had made plans to attack their school, which was located in the Hudson Valley in New York. The plan was to attack on the eleventh anniversary of the Columbine attacks on April 20, 2010, and they posted messages and photos online, detailing what they planned to do, including mapping out and clearly identifying the areas of the school they expected to target. However, another student saw the postings on MySpace and reported it to one of the high school principals. Though the police then searched the school and didn't find any bombs or harmful objects, the three students were arrested and charged with a felony.

A burglar in Loudoun County, Virginia, Mike Swain, stopped in the middle of a home robbery to put in a call to a psychic for advice and ran up a huge phone bill. Too bad he wasn't psychic enough or didn't learn from the psychic that this call would lead the police right to him. This inopportune call happened after the burglar found some valuable objects in the home he was burglarizing and was about to steal even more when he spied a phone and decided to call a psychic—presumably for some advice on where to find more and how to best profit from his new-found success. And for a time it did seem like the burglar had successfully made off with his haul and had gotten some helpful psychic insights in the process.

But then, the homeowner's phone bill arrived later that month, which revealed that the call to the psychic's 900 line had cost $250. After the homeowner saw the huge charge, he called the police, who traced the call back to the psychic. And then, it was just a matter of the psychic checking her records, whereupon she discovered the criminal had used his own real name.

A Florida man was accused of robbing and beating a woman. In the process of robbing her, he stole not only her money, but also her cell phone. When the woman told her boyfriend what had happened, he decided to call the phone. The robber actually answered it, and believed the boyfriend's story when he pretended to be someone who was selling some guns. The two of them set a meeting point, and instead of buying guns, when the thief arrived, he was promptly arrested.

In a text-messaging case, a Salt Lake City detective received an unusual text message on his cell phone from a drug dealer seeking to make a sale who apparently dialed the wrong number. But it was definitely the right number for the detective to make a bust. The message read: "I have 10 Lortab 7.5," and the detective decided to play along to help trap the suspected dealer. He texted back questions asking for a price, time, and place where he could buy the prescription pain medication, and after the dealer responded with the information, police detectives waited for the drug dealer to show up at the Wal-Mart parking lot at 8:00 p.m. Three women showed up with the tablets—Carrie Brooker, 27; Christine Rollins, 42; and one other unidentified woman—and were easily arrested.

A fifteen-year-old teenager in Largo, Florida, stole marine radio equipment, and then used it to place phony Mayday calls to the Coast Guard, costing the government hundreds of thousands of dollars in responding to these calls. The Coast Guard sent out helicopters on at least four occasions to search fruitlessly for a sinking boat or drowning person over a several day period, leading the Coast Guard and Federal Communications Commission to begin still another search—this time for the perpetrator of the hoaxes.

In turn, the teen experienced his own personal Mayday, when his mother found the expensive radio equipment in her son's room, became suspicious, and called the Largo police. One officer went to the house and found two marine radios and four other communication devices, which the teen admitted to stealing from boats. Why? Because, the teen told the police, "He needed something to do." Now he'll probably have plenty to do, though it may be in jail.

A counterfeiter—thirty-five-year-old Michael Jerome Chatman—made the mistake of returning a printer to a clerk at a Target store in Augusta, Georgia. Presumably, he was trying to get his money back for the printer, but instead, when the clerk checked the box, she saw a piece of paper stuck inside the printer. When, she looked more closely, she saw the paper contained copies of a $20 and $10 bill. Chatman then abandoned his plans to try to return the printer and tried to run from the store, but he was stopped outside by a Richmond County deputy, and when the police frisked him, they found a real $20 bill that matched the copy inside the printer. After that, they not only arrested him, but his two accomplices, Diamond Tiara Green, 30, and Kotto Yaphet Green, 24. So instead of making some easy money, they're probably going to be making some hard time in jail.

revor Agnew, a forty-four-year-old burglar from Manchester, England, didn't understand how ATM machines work, which led to his arrest. Agnew broke into several houses and stole ATM cards. However, he wasn't able to easily find out the pin numbers, which he needed to release any money. So, he decided to try to guess the codes. He went to the same ATM machine, which was close to his own house, and tried to guess the number for an ATM card over fifty times, thinking he'd get lucky. But, with over ten thousand code possibilities, he was never able to get any money out. Unfortunately, his repeated failed attempts at the same machine aroused suspicion, and when the photo the police managed to take of him with a security camera was shown on television, someone turned him in.

CHAPTER 11

RETURNING TO THE SCENE OF THE CRIME

Returning to the crime scene is another reason that many criminals screw up. Here are some examples of criminals who violated the "no returns" or "curiosity killed the cat" principle by going back to the scene of the crime.

Two robbers in Dalian, China, wondered whether the shop they had just burglarized had a security camera. They had successfully robbed a customer at a game shop of some cash and his mobile phone, but after the heist, they made a bet about whether the shop had a security camera and decided to go back and check. Then, they agreed, the loser would treat the winner to a visit to a Karaoke bar. Presumably, the man who bet there was a security camera would be delighted to win the bet, but the two robbers both lost, because before they were able to return to check out the shop, the victim had already reported the theft to the police, who had taken a video clip of the robbery from the surveillance camera, and had asked the shop owners to watch for any suspicious gamers. So when the two robbers returned to the shop the next afternoon, all the owner had to do was call the police who arrested the pair for the robbery.

A nother Chinese man who was hungry robbed a cake shop in Changchun city, Jilin Province three times—and the third time was the charm for the police. The first time he came in wielding a knife and demanding some cakes, the manager told the staff to give him some, and he ran off with two cakes. But since the loss was so minor, the manager didn't call the police. However, ten minutes later, the robber returned and he left again with two more cakes, whereupon the manager did call the police. So thirty minutes later, when the robber returned once again, still hungry and demanding two more cakes, the police were already there and quickly arrested him. So why take the cakes? Because he had been hungry, he told the police. Unfortunately, he had struck once too often, and it was three strikes and you're out.

An unemployed robber in Tokyo, Japan, who simply needed cash, similarly pressed his luck too far when he robbed the same convenience store for the third time shortly before dawn. Twice before, the man had held up the same convenience store and had disappeared with cash. The third time, though, when he threatened the employee with a knife and forced him to open the cash register, the police were already there before he could flee, since the store owner had called the police and they were staking out the store waiting for him.

Another three-strikes robber made the mistake of announcing to a convenience store clerk that he was going to come back again after committing two robberies earlier that day—and he did. That's what happened in Fort Collins, Colorado, after the criminal robbed the same 7-Eleven store twice in one day—once in the morning and once in the afternoon. And each time, the clerk gave him what he asked for, according to store policy. But then, as he left after the second robbery, he told the clerk he was coming back to rob the store again later that day, because he wanted to "give the clerk a break in between robberies so there would be more money in the cash register." Makes sense, maybe, but why push your luck by going back to the place a third time, and worse, why tell the clerk you are going to do it? But the dumb robber did, and so when he returned to the 7-Eleven a few hours later, detectives investigating his second robbery were already there and they promptly arrested him—on two counts of robbery for the morning and afternoon successes, and one count of attempted robbery for the third and last attempt.

One robber in West Haven, Connecticut, twenty-four-year-old Kenneth Jeffries, took a pack of gum to the counter and gave the clerk a dollar to pay for it. But after the clerk rang up the purchase, Jeffries pulled out a gun, pointed it at the clerk, and demanded all the money in the register. At once, the clerk gave it to him, and the robber fled with both the money and the gum. However, a few minutes later, Jeffries returned, asking the clerk if he had paid for the gum, He presumably planned to pay for it as a regular purchase, perhaps to assuage his guilty conscience, though he had robbed the store. In any case, the police were already there, since the clerk had called about the robbery, so they quickly arrested him. He had in effect gummed up his own successful robbery from the store.

In another case, the remorse of a robber in Connecticut didn't prevent him from robbing a Subway store twice, though he apologized each time. The first time, he ordered the clerk to hand over the cash, and then told her, "Sorry I have to do this." Then, a week later, when he returned, he ordered the clerk to empty the register, again said he was sorry, and thanked the clerk for the money on his way out. However, this time, the police caught his getaway car, pulled him over, and arrested him.

nother robber entered a restaurant, approached a waitress, and told her to give him all the money in the restaurant. However, the robber used a phony, heavy Cajun accent, and the waitress couldn't understand what he was saying. The robber used the same voice to try to rob one of the customers, but the customer couldn't understand him either. Furious, the robber pulled out his gun, but when he pulled the trigger, the gun wouldn't fire. So instead, he grabbed the cash register and tried to run off with it. But the cash register was still plugged into the wall, and after the robber ran a few feet, he ran out of cord, and as the register was jerked out of his hands, he fell to the floor. So feeling frustrated and humiliated, he fled from the café, while someone put the cash register back on the counter. However, rather than go somewhere else after his spectacularly bad defeat, he returned five minutes later, his gun drawn, and this time, he unplugged the cash register before fleeing again. But he didn't get very far, since one of the patrons who had seen his previous performance stepped up to him, knocked him down, and made a citizen's arrest, holding the robber there until the police arrived to take him away.

Jeremy Hart, 24, entered an unlocked home after he crashed his Oldsmobile Cutlass into a snow bank outside a home, broke into the home, and stole prescription medicines and votive candles. Though the homeowners were awakened by their barking dog and then heard footsteps, they didn't want to go downstairs and confront any intruder. But they did see Hart from a window once he was outside, and they called the police.

Still, Hart might have been able to get away, except for his broken-down car. As a result, after about five minutes, a shivering Hart left his car and knocked on the door of the house he had just burglarized. Then, he explained to the owner that he was sorry to disturb him, but his car had broken down and he was cold. Though the owner was suspicious about the close timing between the burglary and knock on the door, he let Hart in, and when a police officer arrived a few minutes later, Hart was conveniently still there. Though the homeowners hadn't seen Hart in their house, Kaminski found the stolen candles in Hart's car, and he arrested Hart for operating a vehicle under the influence, as well as for the burglary. So now Hart will have a chance to warm up at the local jail.

C alling for help from tech support on an item you have stolen is also not a good idea. That's what happened when thirty-three-year-old Timothy Scott Short stole a PC and a Digimarc printer used to print driver's licenses from a contract office of the Missouri Department of Revenue. The owner was a subcontractor for the Department who had the right to print drive's licenses. However, the printer was locked with a key stored in a secure location, so it couldn't be used to print licenses as the robber had planned.

But Short thought he could be smart by calling the Digimarc Company's tech support line two days later with his request to buy printer drivers for the model of the printer he had stolen. In his call, he not only used his real name, but he also gave Digimarc the same phone number he had used in an unrelated identity theft case. As a result, when a Secret Service agent later listened to a recording of Short's call for help, he recognized Short's voice from a prior investigation, leading to his arrest for the stolen equipment and a potential ten-year sentence in prison.

One homeowner experienced three break-ins in the same number of months. The home was in an isolated area with no streetlights, so the homeowner bought a gun to protect himself from any future burglaries. As a result, when one burglar broke his living room window and climbed in, Rob, who heard the noise, was inside waiting for him. Rob stepped out from behind the wall, pointed the gun, and said, "You're a dead man." In response, the would-be burglar gave out a loud scream, dove through the window, and took off running. In fact, he ran so fast, he left his car in the driveway, still running, providing the police with helpful assistance in tracking him down.

Alton Tillman, an eighty-five-year-old man in Clovis, New Mexico, successfully confronted a burglar after his home was burglarized three times in a week. He led the burglar to believe that he had left for the day by leaving his home at his regular time on a Tuesday, but then he doubled back and quietly went inside. There he found emptied drawers and items strewn all over the floor and someone's feet sticking out from under the bed. Tillman, holding a gun, ordered the man to get out, and called 911. When the officers arrived soon after that, Tillman was still pointing a handgun at the sixteen-year-old boy who was standing against the wall, and after checking the boy's pockets, they found several items belonging to Tillman.

Two other burglars, Robert Garrett, 33, and Jesse Dyer, 32, were arrested in Lincoln, Nebraska, after stealing a fifty-five-inch television. With difficulty, they carried the heavy television to their getaway car, only to realize that it wouldn't fit into the trunk or through a door. When a next-door neighbor spotted them, they paid her $100 and asked her to hold the set until they could return with a bigger car. Instead, she called the police, who arrested Garrett and Dyer when they returned to pick up the stolen property.

A bank robbery suspect in Grand Rapids, Michigan, decided to hold up the same credit union twice in one month. While his first robbery seemed to be successful, he didn't even make it inside the bank for the second one. As he approached the West Michigan Credit Union on foot, a worker thought he was the same guy who held up the bank three weeks before. So the employees locked the door before he could get inside and called the police. Seeing that his do it again approach wasn't going to work, the man headed back to his car and got in. But before he could drive away, the police stopped him and arrested him, initially for the earlier robbery. After all, he hadn't even gotten into the bank the second time. But on interrogation, he confessed not only to the previous robbery but to planning to hold up the credit union again.

CHAPTER 12

CALLING THE LAW FOR HELP

Another big mistake many stupid criminals make is when they think they're smarter than the police, and file a report about a crime they actually committed, thinking that they'll get away with it. Or, they make the mistake of dialing 911 when they mean to call another number.

Curtiss Randall Coleman of Escatawpa, Mississippi, mistakenly called 911 instead of 411 when he was trying to find the number for Biloxi's WLOX-TV to complain about not getting a FEMA trailer after Hurricane Katrina. When he reached the emergency dispatcher by mistake, he simply hung up without saying anything. Unfortunately for him, the Jackson County Sheriff's Department sent deputies to the home he called from to see if anyone needed assistance. Coleman didn't answer the door when the police knocked, hoping the officers might go away. He didn't have any such luck. Instead, the officers broke down his front door, and discovered what appeared to be a methamphetamine lab in the home. Coleman and his thirty-year-old son were promptly arrested.

A San Mateo County, California inmate who walked away from a minimum security jail during a work release program also got into trouble for dialing 911. The man escaped from the jail and started walking. However, he soon tired and decided to phone a friend to pick him up. He stopped at a pay phone and tried to dial 411 since he couldn't remember his friend's phone number. Unfortunately for him, he dialed 911 instead. While he hung up as soon as the emergency dispatcher answered, it was already too late. At once, the dispatcher sent out an officer to check on the 911 call, and the officer found the man still sitting in the phone booth and still wearing his shirt from prison that announced that it was the property of the San Mateo County Honor Camp.

While misdialing 411 is a common reason for calling 911, two suspects in Pomona, California found another reason—typing in 911 into a cell phone pager to indicate to the person on the other side that the call is urgent. That's what two suspects did when they were trying to page a drug dealer from a pay phone and added 911 to their paged phone message to tell the dealer they wanted to make an urgent dope deal. However, instead of paging their dealer, they managed to call 911 instead, and officers were sent to their location. When the police arrived, they found the two suspects, Paul White and Ryan Ogie, in a car with stolen plates, and inside, they found suspected burglary tools. White and Ogie were quickly placed under arrest.

R eporting the theft of marijuana to the police is a dumb move, especially when you're in the country illegally. That's what Jose Guadalupe Flores, 35, did after two masked gunmen invaded his home in South Texas by kicking in the door, ransacking the house, and stealing one hundred fifty pounds of marijuana, while Flores fled. Apparently, Flores had found a lucrative business in packing and shipping marijuana, and he had been wrapping the drugs to send out when the burglars arrived. But things got even worse for Flores when he walked into the local police station and told deputies how he had been wrapping the drugs for shipment and how the men stole his marijuana. After the sheriff's deputies went to his house to investigate, they found nearly fifteen pounds of pot still on the floor, and they arrested Flores for felony possession of marijuana. Plus, since Flores was an illegal immigrant from Mexico, he was held in jail until his case was heard. And the two gunmen? The police were still searching for them, while Flores remained in jail.

C alling 911 and filing a false police report can lead to trouble, as three drug trafficking suspects—ages 17, 29, and 31—found out when they were caught with drugs after a routine traffic stop in Canada. While speaking to the men through the driver's-side car window, the officer smelled a strong marijuana odor coming out of the car, so the officer asked the driver to get out of the car for further questioning. Meanwhile, the other two suspects remained in the car. As the questioning continued, the police suddenly received a 911 call in which a male caller reported a robbery in progress at a local bank.

But if the suspects in the car though that a report of a nearby bank robbery might get them off the hook, it only dug them in deeper. Other officers handled the bank call and quickly determined the report was false, while the officers at the car continued their investigation and found more than eleven kilograms of marijuana in the car, and arrested the suspects for possessing a controlled substance. Later, the officers determined that the false 911 call reporting the bank robbery came from one of the suspect's cell phones, leading to additional criminal charges being filed against the suspect.

In a similar case, a Sarasota, Florida, man tried to make a fake 911 call to get rid of the police. The twenty-eight-year-old man was being followed by police who were trying to pull him over for a routine traffic stop. When he saw they were behind him, he made a 911 call to report an armed robbery in progress several blocks away. While his plan seemed to work at first, when the officers turned around and headed toward the bank, other officers in the area soon were back to following the man and trying to pull him over. When they finally pulled him over, they discovered a gun in his car, which he wasn't allowed to carry because he was a felon, and the criminal charges against him intensified when they discovered that he made the false 911 call.

Police investigated a call from a shopping mall, which reported that a purse had been stolen after a clerk noticed it missing and their security tape showed a man stealing it from a display. Other thefts by the same person were also reported by other stores. When the police arrested a suspect, Parris Phillips, but discovered he didn't have the purse, the police reviewed the security tapes again and found that he was working with at least one woman, and the police released a description of her.

After the description was released, three women—Denise Lewis, Asa Cox, and Alexsandra Selmon—lost their car in the shopping mall. They had been using the car to hide items they had been stealing—along with Phillips—from the various high-end retailers located in the mall, so it was probably a bad idea that they approached a police officer to help them find their car. When the police officer saw the women, he recognized one matching the description of the woman

who had been seen on the surveillance tape working with Phillips, so the officer arrested all three women. The police did eventually find their car in the parking lot, and the missing $10,000 purse on the backseat. Then, when the police searched the car, they found dozens of other items worth thousands of dollars that had also been stolen from the mall, along with wire cutters and a utility knife which the thieves used to cut off security tags.

Daniel Cabral was arrested and charged with burglarizing a building at the University of Massachusetts–Dartmouth, but gave the police a false address to thrown them off his trail. However, as he was going home after his arraignment, he was robbed at gunpoint, and when he reported the crime to police, he provided his real address. While the police were quite helpful in arresting the three people suspected of robbing him, they also got a search warrant for Cabral's real home address, where they found the computer equipment that had been taken from the university, along with power tools that had been stolen from a local theater.

A sking the police for help when the car you just stole goes into a ditch is also not a good idea. That's what happened to Dean Gangle, 40, of Richmond, Minnesota, when he crashed a stolen car into a ditch by the side of a country road in the middle of the night. But rather than leaving it there and escaping, he stayed by the car and flagged down a passing motorist for help in pulling the car out of the ditch. Unfortunately, the helpful motorist who stopped to help him at 4:45 a.m. turned out to be an off-duty sheriff's deputy on his way home, The deputy noticed that the car in the ditch matched the description of one reported stolen several hours earlier in a nearby town. After the deputy called dispatchers on his radio and they confirmed it was the stolen car, the deputy placed Gangle under arrest.

R.C. Gaitlin, 21, walked up to two patrol officers in Detroit, who were showing their squad car computer equipment to children in the neighborhood. He was curious how the system worked, and when he asked the officers, they asked him for a piece of identification. Big mistake. When they entered his name into the computer, the information on the screen showed that Gaitlin was wanted for a two-year old armed robbery charge in St. Louis, Missouri. So, instead of explaining the technology, the police officers placed him under arrest.

Three car thieves managed to turn themselves in when one of them accidently dialed 911 on his cell phone. When the Orange County, California, police dispatcher answered the 911 call, he heard what sounded like an ongoing robbery. The dispatcher got in touch with the police and dispatched them to the scene after finding the thieves' location using cellular phone pinpointing technology. The police quickly arrived on the scene and arrested the men.

CHAPTER 13

BAD HIDING PLACES

Another common mistake criminals make is finding a bad hiding place when they try to escape. Sometimes the hiding place itself a giveaway, and sometimes the hiding place is too uncomfortable or painful to endure.

Sometimes closets can be good hiding places, but not if you decide to hide where the victim is already hiding from you, as three burglars—Adam Cloward, Jake Hampton, and Tony Cone—discovered in West Jordan, Utah. As they broke into a home, the terrified twenty-one-year-old victim, Brittany, heard the window shatter, grabbed her cell phone, ran upstairs, jumped into a closet to hide from the intruders, and called 911.

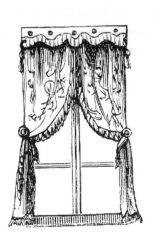

Meanwhile, not even realizing she was there, they proceeded to ransack the house, searching for valuables, and eventually went upstairs and entered the same room where Brittany was hiding. She could even see them through the slats of the closet as they searched. Just then, the police arrived on the scene, and hearing them, one of the men jumped into the closet to hide, standing right next to Brittany, though still not realizing she was there. But then, as Brittany heard the police come into the room, she screamed out, "He's in here!" and moments later the police rushed in and arrested the man in the closet, as well as his two accomplices.

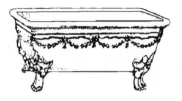

A hot tub may not make the best hiding place either, as a mail thief, Mathew Keuscher, discovered when he tried to hide in one in Hillsboro, Oregon. The incident began when Washington County deputies approached Keuscher as he sat in his car and noticed he had other people's mail inside the car. But before the officers could question him, he got out of the car, ran off, and managed to lose the officers by running into the backyard of a nearby house. As the police continued their search with a police dog, a neighbor heard some banging and then a loud thump as the lid on his outdoor hot tub closed. He reported the strange noise to the police officers, and within minutes they found the suspect in the hot tub and arrested him.

One bank robber in Wilmington, Delaware, tried to hide in the locked, glass-enclosed entrance of an office building. The police were searching the area around the bank for the suspect, and they quickly spotted him behind the clear glass.

One robber jumped off a bridge in an attempt to escape his pursuers. Unfortunately for the man, he jumped into a shallow river, broke his leg, and was unable to move until the police searching for him found him, still holding the bag with his ill-gotten goods.

One robber climbed up a tree in the middle of a golf course to hide from the police who were searching for him. However, instead of keeping quiet to avoid being found, he helpfully called down to a golfer where he would be able to find his golf ball, and the golfer turned him over to the police.

Roger Golden, a New York City drug smuggler, put thirty-five pounds of marijuana in the locker of a self-storage facility. However, the facility had two entrances—one of them located in the lobby of the Drug Enforcement Administration building. When the drug agents walked by on their way to work, they could smell the marijuana, and they quickly returned with a drug-sniffing dog, who headed directly for Golden's locker. Needless to say, Golden was soon placed under arrest for drug possession.

CHAPTER 14

BAD COMPANIONS

Another common reason that criminals get caught is because they are turned in by their own partners in crime or by others who know them.

One thief decided to steal a ring from a jewelry store, so he could give his girlfriend a present on her birthday. Unfortunately for the thief, his girlfriend was the owner of the jewelry store he robbed, and as soon as she opened her gift, she recognized the stolen ring and called the police.

A twenty-four-year-old from Quebec tried to use a siphon hose to steal a tank of gasoline from another person's car. As his two accomplices watched, he drained the gas, but then discovered that he could not get the hose out of the tank. He stuck his finger in the tank to try to loosen the hose, but his finger got stuck in the spring-loaded device inside of the tank. Not knowing who else to call, his two accomplices dialed 911 and fled the scene, leaving their friend literally stuck for the crime after neither the paramedics nor the police could free him. Eventually, firefighters arrived and were able to cut out part of the gas tank and free him. After a quick trip to the hospital, he was quickly arrested and convicted.

It's not a good idea to have a fight with your crime partner in the middle of trying to commit the crime, as a young couple discovered when they tried to hold up a bank in Ishioka, Japan. The seventeen-year-old-boy and sixteen-year-old girl arrived at the bank, waving around kitchen knives. But when the boy walked up to a customer at the bank and held up the knife, the man walked away, and when the boy turned to the teller waving his knife at her, she seemed similarly unimpressed. At this point, the girl began berating the boy for his ineffective efforts, whereupon the two began arguing back and forth, and were so embroiled in fighting with each other, that they didn't notice when one of the tellers tripped the bank's silent alarm. As a result, the police were soon on the scene, while the couple still were fighting. While the boy was still making threats with his knife and begging anyone to give him some money, his girlfriend was yelling at him to hurry up.

— CHAPTER 15 —

ENCOUNTERS WITH
THE VICTIM

Even when crooks think they have gotten away, they may fall into a trap when the victim later sees them and chases them down or calls the police. Sometimes, though, the criminal is just plain stupid and uses the stolen items too soon and too close to the scene of the crime.

One purse snatcher in Bari, Italy, made the mistake of unknowingly trying to rob his own mother. The man sped down the street on his motorcycle, driving past a woman on foot, reached over, and grabbed her purse off of her shoulder. When he turned around to look back at his victim, he saw that the stunned woman was his own mother. Needless to say, she had no trouble identifying him to the police, whom she quickly called to report the crime.

In another case, a forty-one-year-old man in Cobb County, Georgia, held up a Race Trac gas station, waving a gun, and using a piece of cloth thrown over his face as his disguise. Unfortunately for him, the cloth only covered part of his face, so the clerk on duty at the gas station—who ended up being his daughter—was able to recognize him, identify him for the police, and tell them exactly where he lived after he fled the scene.

Christopher Paul Stafford, 25, stole a red and silver bike worth about $900, which had been parked in front of a convenience store. Five days later, he rode the bike back to the scene of his crime, where the cashier of the convenience store—the real owner of the bike—spotted it and called the police who easily made their arrest.

In another case, a jewel thief made the mistake of trying to sell some stolen jewelry back to the store owner he originally stole it from. The incident started when the thief went to an antique show in Miami, Florida, where dozens of exhibitors were displaying their expensive merchandise. Then, attracted to a beautiful $3,200 watch, when no one was paying attention, he quietly picked it up and slipped into his pocket. The thief thought he would be able to sell the watch for some easy money, and picked a random antique store in the area where he tried to sell the watch. However, as soon as he walked into the store, he realized he had made a big mistake. Behind the counter was the same woman who was working at the booth from which he had stolen the watch. She recognized him and started yelling, and the other customers quickly surrounded him and physically held him in the store until the police arrived to arrest him.

A postal worker from Detroit, Michigan, was charged with stealing gold from the mail after he tried to sell it back to the very same shop that had shipped it. The postal worker stole the gold from the mail, took it to G&S Brokers pawnshop, and sold it for $320. The jeweler recognized the gold—which he himself had melted down and mailed to a business in Ann Arbor.

In a similar case, a thief in Germany stole a collection of extremely valuable, rare coins. He decided to take them to a bank for safe-keeping until he decided how to sell them. However, soon after he made the deposit, a bank vault employee who was in charge of locking up deposits in the vault, recognized them as the $80,000 set of coins that had been stolen from his home a short time earlier. Police were able to track down the thirty-six-year-old thief and arrest him, and the bank employee got his collection returned to him.

Jimmy Leeroy Walker twice robbed the Sunshine Car Wash in Clearwater, Florida, around Christmas time, neither time bothering to disguise his face. The first time, he smashed a side window to get in, and then proceeded to steal money out of the cash register. The second time he broke in, he only managed to steal a tip jar with $9 in it. Then, a few days later, Walker returned to Sunshine Car Wash and dropped of an employment application. Unfortunately for him, the manager recognized him and called the police.

A would-be robber entered Charlie's Supermarket, a grocery store in Jacksonville, Florida. The thief entered the store with a paper bag over his head, with eyeholes cut out. When he confronted the clerk to demand money, the bag on his head shifted, and not only could he no longer see, the clerk couldn't hear what he was saying, since his words were muffled by the paper bag. When the thief tried to fix the problem by cutting another hole in the bag for his mouth, he cut the bag too much, and the entire bag split open. Immediately, the clerk could see his face, and recognized him as a regular at the store, and was able to identify him to the police after the thief fled. His capture was literally in the bag.

In Wichita, Kansas, a woman came to the back door of a local fast-food restaurant, and when the waitress came out with her order, she wielded a gun and demanded money. Unfortunately, the waitress recognized the woman with the gun—she had stopped by the restaurant earlier that day to apply for a job there and had spoken to the waitress for quite a while.

CHAPTER 16

SHOW OFF

Sometimes crooks get done in by their vanity. They have a desire to show off or they wear something to the crime that turns into a big giveaway because they are wearing something that gives away who they are.

One night, an armed and masked burglar broke into a store that sold T-shirts. Before leaving, he saw a video camera that would transfer an image of one's face onto a T-shirt and decided to get one for himself. However, the camera not only recorded his face allowing the police to know who to look for, but when the police caught up with him, he was wearing the T-shirt.

Donna Lee Sobb won $100 in the California state lottery, which qualified her for the state's $2 million jackpot. Besides needing the money, she was delighted to when the local newspaper printed an article about her and featured her photograph. However, before she had too much time to bask in the glow of celebrity, a city police offer saw her picture in the paper, and realized her photo was in the police files as well. Sobb was wanted on a shoplifting warrant issued eight months earlier, and she was promptly arrested.

Two men in Fort Lauderdale, Florida—twenty-year-old Charles V. Podesta Jr. and nineteen-year-old Karl F. Kuhn II—posted a video on MySpace of themselves online harassing a manatee, a rare aquatic mammal. Unfortunately for Podesta and Kuhn, the manatee is on Florida's endangered species list, and when the local authorities saw the video, the two were arrested and sent to jail for violating the Endangered Species Act.

In another case, a man made the mistake of posting a video of himself with a stolen police Taser gun on YouTube. The video star, a twenty-two-year-old man, stole the Taser from the squad car of an East Troy, Wisconsin police officer. He probably would have gotten away with it if he hadn't posted the video online. And, when the police saw the video, it was easy for them to find him, since he was already in their custody on an unrelated matter.

nother YouTube video turned a $15 prank into jail time for a Los Angeles man and two teenage friends. The caper started when Robert Echeverria, 32, and his friends filmed and posted a video to YouTube called "How to Scam Del Taco," which showed how to easily obtain bags of tacos and quesadillas from the fast-food restaurant. In the video, Echeverria calls Del Taco from his car and amiably says he's Robert

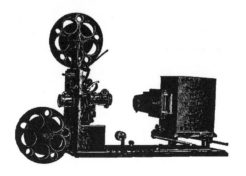

Kennedy, a company CEO, who has "already spoken to the store's manager and corporate office about some unwanted sour cream and the lack of a receipt in a previous order," and concludes by saying "I love your guys' tacos." Then, the ploy having worked, the video filmed by eighteen-year-old Ian Roman shows eighteen-year-old costar, Brian Fawcett, going into the restaurant and picking up the food—two quesadillas with extra chicken, seven tacos, two sodas, and a large order of fries. After that, the three men can be seen enjoying their feast and laughing, as the video ends, with two of Echeverria's phone numbers posted across the screen in case anyone wants to get in touch. After one viewer saw the video, he called the police, who easily found the three men, and arrested all three.

A former California gang member wrote about his involvement in a jewelry robbery in his published memoirs. As he described in bragging detail, he had been the mastermind behind the plot and was the gang's getaway driver. Now that he was no longer a member of the gang involved in crime, he must have thought he could talk openly about what he did way back when. Unfortunately for him, once the local police read about his crime in his memoirs, they arrested him and the prosecutors used his book as evidence against him during the trial. Afterward, he was sentenced to prison for his role as the heist's mastermind and driver of the getaway car.

A suspected thief, Jose Perez, wore some jewelry that he stole from a booth at a jewelry display in Bryant Park in New York City. He lifted the jewelry—a citrine pendant and an amethyst ring—from the Dazzler Studios booth on Sunday, and then made the mistake of wearing the two items to the park the following day. The jeweler, Susan Manley, who was staffing the booth saw him as he walked by, and after she notified a nearby maintenance worker, he radioed for security and trailed the man to a nearby Japanese restaurant. Then, when the police arrive, the security guard pointed him out and the police arrested Perez for grand larceny. Not only was wearing the two pieces of stolen jewelry, but he also had a jacket and duffel bag full of more jewelry and some videotapes he had stolen, as well.

A robber who turned up at court in the boots he had stolen made a similar mistake. The robber had committed the crime when he confronted a clerk with a knife and demanded all the money in the cash register. However, the $69 wasn't enough, so as he left, he grabbed a pair of tan hiking boots. Though he was later arrested and held for trial, the prosecutors had little evidence, other than the clerk's claim that this was the man who robbed her. As the trial proceeded, even though the clerk said she was certain that the defendant was the robber, there was no other evidence and it looked like the jury wasn't convinced of the accused's guilt. But then, the defendant cockily put his feet on the table and leaned back, feeling confident in his impending acquittal. However, he was wearing the tan boots he had stolen, and the clerk immediately identified them. It was all the jury needed to convince them. Within minutes, the jury found the defendant guilty of aggravated robbery, and not only did the bailiff take him away, but the judge confiscated his boots, so he walked on to jail in his socks.

In Tempe, Arizona, a seventeen-year-old broke into an apartment bedroom at Arizona State University. He managed to steal several hundred dollars in miscellaneous items and cash before falling asleep on the bedroom floor. That's where a female student found him after she woke up at 5 a.m. He quickly fled the scene, and while the victim didn't get a clear look at his face, she did see the monkey-print pajamas that he was wearing. As a result of the description she gave the police, a Tempe police officer thought it sounded like a person the police had previously had contact with, and headed to the man's apartment. Though the man pretended to be asleep, the police entered his apartment where they found him wearing the monkey pajamas and arrested him. You might say the man made a monkey of himself—and the police weren't about to let him make a monkey of them.

——CHAPTER 17——

REVELATIONS

Besides showing off, criminals reveal themselves in other ways, such as bragging about the crime, confessing, or even using obvious evidence of the crime in daily life.

A man was arrested and questioned about a string of vending machine break-ins. At first, the police didn't have enough evidence to charge him with the crime, but when he paid his $400 bail entirely in quarters, the police questioned him further about where he got so many quarters, and finally got him to confess.

Two men in the Southwest were being tried for armed robbery and assault. As the prosecutor questioned the victim who had been with her husband when they were robbed at gunpoint by two men, he asked if the two men who committed this crime were in the courtroom. But before the victim could answer, the two defendants raised their hands.

In another case in Newport Beach, California, police had someone in custody who they suspected of being involved in the robbery of a jewelry store. They found his wallet in the getaway car, but they couldn't actually place him at the scene of the crime. In fact, the suspect was denying every having been to Newport Beach. While watching the security videos from the jewelry store of the day before the robbery, the police see a grainy figure that they think might be their suspect. However, the picture is too unclear for them to make a positive identification. The detectives take the video to their suspect asking him to look at it. After watching the video for a while, when the grainy image of the suspicious-looking man comes onto the screen, the suspect blurts out: "Damn, that's me!"

An inmate serving time for one crime made the mistake of calling the prosecutor's office to ask whether or not he was being prosecuted for another crime. At the time he made the phone call, he was serving a ten-year sentence for robbing a gas station. Before he had started serving his time, though, he had been arrested and charged with a bank robbery, but the case had never been prosecuted since the file was misplaced. Unfortunately, his call rescued his long-dormant case, which was actually about to expire. As a result, the prosecutor quickly filed new charges, and the criminal ended up serving an additional ten years in prison.

Quinton J. Thomas, 22, was in jail, accused of planning a robbery and killing someone while committing the crime. His attorney had urged Thomas to plead guilty because the evidence against him seemed so bad. But Thomas wasn't about to plead guilty. Instead, he wrote a letter to a friend of his. In it, he told his friend to keep two of the prosecution's witnesses from testifying, and provided some information on how he was going to falsely explain away some of the evidence against him. However, the letter was returned to the sender and opened by the jail employees conducting a search of incoming mail for contraband. The letter was all the prosecutor needed to finish the case. Not only did he go after Thomas for the charges in the original indictment—first degree murder, attempted armed robbery, and conspiracy to commit armed robbery—but he added three new charges—solicitation to commit murder and two counts of witness intimidation. After seven hours of deliberation, the jury found Thomas guilty on all counts.

Christopher Kron from Naples, Florida, broke into a restaurant, which activated an alarm. When the alarm company called the store, the burglar answered the phone and gave the operator his real name, but couldn't tell her the pass code needed to turn off the alarm. A review of the video surveillance by the alarm company showed a man walking around the bar area before leaving the building holding what looked like a liquor bottle. Even with identifying himself honestly to the security operator, he still might have gotten away with his crime. However, the next morning, he returned to the restaurant where an employee recognized him and called the police.

Writing a stick-up note on the back of your own check is also a sure ticket to jail. That's what happened to a bank robber in Englewood, Colorado, when he walked into a bank, pulled out one of his own checks, scratched out his own name on the front, and scrawled his note demanding cash on the back. Then, priding himself for a successful robbery, he left with $5,000 in cash. But what he didn't notice was that he hadn't scratched out his name very well, so anyone who looked closely at the check that he left behind with the bank teller, including the police, could easily read it. Soon after he returned home, the police arrived to make the arrest.

Melanie Brockway, 23, from Philadelphia also left identification behind at the scene of her crime. The young woman was suspected of vandalizing several buildings with graffiti, but no one could prove it. However, on one of her last buildings, she included her MySpace account name "Devient Art" within the graffiti. Using the name and the account, the police were able to track her down and arrest her.

Another young man drove away from police officers who stopped him, but made the mistake of handing over his drivers license first. The thirty-two-year-old man was pulled over at a sobriety checkpoint in Portsmouth, New Hampshire, and handed over his license and registration. Then, suddenly, with his identification cards still in the officer's hand, he hit the gas and sped away, almost hitting another officer with his car. Police easily caught up with him since they knew his name and where he lived from the license, and found him in possession of marijuana.

Writing a stick-up note on the back of a police report about your own previous arrest is also not a smart move. But that's what bank robber Osman S. Brown 19, did in Jacksonville, Florida, when he robbed the First Union Bank around 11:00 a.m. one morning. Wearing blue jeans, a T-shirt, and carrying a Starter jacket, he walked into the bank and handed the teller a note, which he had written on the back of a December 15 arrest report describing how he was charged with opposing a police officer by yelling at him and becoming physically aggressive. In the note, he wrote that he had several pounds of explosives with him. Though he never actually showed the teller the explosives, the teller handed over some cash, and Brown fled to his home a half-dozen blocks from the bank. He never got there. Using the address on the police report he left behind with the teller, the police were able to find him walking down the street halfway between the bank and his home.

One safecracker in Indiana broke into a small business that commonly had several thousand dollars in cash in its safe. The safecracker was confident about being successful in breaking into the safe because it was an older model, and the company had no burglar alarms, so he'd have plenty of time. However, after he entered the building, he discovered a few video surveillance cameras. Not wanting to be observed, he decided to disable the cameras. He found a ladder, climbed up, and removed each camera lens. However, while he was unscrewing the lenses from the cameras, unbeknownst to him, they took close-ups of his face.

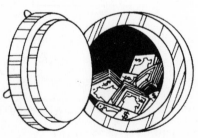

A twenty-nine-year-old drug dealer from Galveston, Texas, made the job of arresting him very easy for the police. Acting on a tip he received, a police officer called a cell phone number and pretended that he was in the market for some cocaine. The person who answered the phone agreed to sell it to them, and the police officer asked the dealer to meet him at a specific address to finish the sale, and to describe himself so the undercover officer would know how to recognize him. After the drug dealer specifically described himself and drove to the meeting point, he was promptly arrested.

CHAPTER 18

KEYSTONE CRIMINALS

The Keystone Cops were a staple of silent Hollywood films, known for their bumbling and incompetence. That's what some criminals are like—they pull out a gun and end up shooting themselves; they stab themselves; they get stuck trying to get over a fence; they shoot themselves in the foot.

It's not a good idea to try to rob a store when the police are there, and it's also not a good idea to run up to a fence if you can't climb over it. That's exactly what Robert Carl Davis tried to do in Sioux Falls, Iowa. One early March morning, he went into the Get-N-Go convenience store, where several police officers were getting their morning cup of coffee. Apparently not aware of the presence of the police, he went over to the counter, pulled out a butterfly knife and waved it at the cashier, cursing at her and demanding money from the register. Hearing the commotion, the police turned and saw Davis at the counter, and as the police advanced toward him, Davis threatened them with his knife. Davis then fled on foot, with the police right behind him. Unfortunately his path was obstructed by a six-foot fence. He attempted to climb over it, but failed, and the police easily arrested him. He'll probably see lots of other fences that he can imagine climbing where he's going now.

At least the robber who failed to climb over the fence didn't get stuck on it, as one criminal did. This is the situation one unfortunate thief found himself in when his feet became impaled on a fence in downtown Durban, South Africa, after he tried to steal goods from informal traders there. He tried to get away by climbing over a palisade fence, when both of his feet got impaled on the fence's large metal rods. Though he managed to get one foot free, he wasn't able to free the other one, and he ended up hanging from the fence for nearly twelve hours, before firefighters and paramedics arrived on the scene to free him. Oddly, the paramedics found him with an unlit cigarette hanging from his lips, since during the night, someone apparently felt sorry enough for him to give him a cigarette, though no one ever offered him a light. After his foot was finally freed, he was taken to Addington hospital for treatment, and then to the police station.

A nother criminal ended his criminal career when he got stuck in a vent shaft. Adam F. Cooper, 19, squeezed into the vent shaft between the ceiling and roof of the grocery store he planned to rob and got stuck. Scared, he screamed for help until someone heard him. Ironically, earlier that day Cooper had been in the vent as part of a team that was cleaning it. In any case, he was fortunate that someone heard him screaming after about an hour, and when emergency workers arrived, they cut away his sweatshirt and poured some vegetable oil from a store shelf to free him. Then, they handed him a rope, and four men standing on the roof pulled him out. After being freed, the police arrested him and he was held on $10,000 bail.

Another criminal was arrested in Des Plaines, Illinois, when he also got caught in a vent shaft. The would-be robber tried to enter a restaurant through its kitchen exhaust vent, but it was too small. Instead of breaking in, he ended up stuck in the exhaust vent, hanging upside down, and covered in grease for twenty-six hours. It turns out that he was lucky to be found when he was, or he could have had a very different ending than arrest. The restaurant had gone out of business. Luckily for the criminal, the owner of the building stopped by to get the mail and found the thief dangling from the shaft.

Blake Leak, a twenty-three-year-old homeless man with twenty-four prior arrests, burglarized a south-side mini-mart in Ossining, New York. He broke in around 3:30 a.m., and after a neighbor called the police to report what he described as "a crashing sound at the store," they arrived while Leak was still in the store. Seeing the police, Leak ran off, though he certainly chose an odd place for his escape, since he ran to the nearby Sing Sing Correctional Facility, where a guard grabbed him and turned him over to police who placed him under arrest.

Eighteen-year old Cheyanne Dwiggins stuffed so many items into her pants when she was shoplifting that when she got into a scuffle with the suspicious store manager, her pants dropped to her ankles. It turns out she had a dozen items in her pants including, several pieces of candy, a potato peeler, an ice cream scoop, a set of measuring spoons, two cake decorating gel tubes, and a can of Nesquik.

Jennifer Hunt, 35, parked her car in a church parking lot early one morning in Athens, Tennessee, and walked around to the back of the church. When the McMinn County Sheriff's deputy, Rick Shadrick, drove by and spotted the lone car parked near the building, he pulled into the parking lot to check on it. The deputy saw Hunt walking out from behind the building and asked her for identification. Unfortunately for Hunt, a crowbar fell out of her pants, and after some further investigation where Shadrick found pry marks on the church doors, he arrested her. You might say this is an example of from crowbars to bars.

Roy Travis Aguilar, 21, was arrested in Santa Fe, New Mexico, for driving while intoxicated, among other charges. The police received a tip over the phone that there was a potentially drunk driver on the highway. A police officer spotted Aguilar's vehicle, swerving across multiple lanes and changing speeds very quickly. When the officer tried to pull him over, he wouldn't stop. Eventually, Aguilar drove his car through a ditch and crashed into a barbed-wire fence. He tried to put his car into park so he could exit the vehicle, but because he was so drunk, he mistakenly put the car into reverse, tried to step out of the car through the open driver's door anyway, and promptly ran over both of his legs. The police put him under arrest and took him to the hospital for treatment.

A man in Leavenworth, Kansas, tried to break into an ATM machine, but ended up seriously injuring himself in the process. The forty-nine-year-old man stole a skid loader, pried a three thousand pound ATM machine loose from outside a credit union early one morning, and attempted to drop it down a fifty-foot cliff, trying to get it to shatter so he could collect the money it held. Unfortunately, when he tried to drop the machine, the skid loader, with the thief still inside, went over the edge as well. The man was freed from the machine, and promptly arrested and taken to the hospital for treatment.

Another pair of criminals managed to steal a bag of rolls at the Cuckoo Restaurant in a suburb of Melbourne, Australia. Initially, the pair—Donna Hayes, 26, and Benjamin Jorgensen, 36—expected to escape with $30,000 in cash, but in the course of the bungled holdup, Jorgensen accidentally blasted Hayes in the hip with a sawed-off shotgun as they tried to flee. Hayes had to spend four weeks in the hospital recovering from her injury, and they were both arrested.

When Kelvin Ethelbert Roberts, 28, tried to rob Gasland USA, a convenience store in Cherryville, North Carolina, he dropped his .45-caliber handgun in front of the store, and when it hit the ground, it fired, and the bullet struck Roberts in the right foot. But even if his injured foot prevented the robbery, the police still had enough evidence to arrest him and charge him with attempted robbery with a dangerous weapon and with possession of a weapon of mass destruction, since the handgun had been altered so it could fire .410 shotgun shells.

Derrick Kosch, 25, entered the Village Pantry, a convenience store in Kokomo, Indiana, with a semiautomatic handgun and ordered the clerk to give him cash and a pack of cigarettes. Obediently, the clerk put the cash in a bag, and was turning to get the cigarettes, when Kosch put the gun into the waistband of his pants, and the gun went off. Though the clerk wasn't injured, the bullet went through his right testicle and lower left leg.

S imilarly, another robber in Baltimore, Maryland, shot himself in the crotch when he attempted to rob a small convenience store. The robber charged through the door of the convenience store, brandishing a semiautomatic handgun, and demanding cash and cigarettes. When the clerk turned around to get the cigarettes, the robber shoved the gun into the waistband of his pants, the trigger got caught, and the blast blew a hole through his testicles and lower left leg. Though he somehow managed to escape, the police found him at home soon after, nursing his wounds.

As funny as some of these stories might be, sometimes the conclusion is quite deadly, which happened to one man in Pinole, California, who died trying to rob a liquor store, when he accidentally shot himself in the leg. The incident occurred when the robber, twenty-four-year-old Sharffeequa Williams, was putting his handgun in the waistband of his pants and the gun went off. He and his accomplice fled in a dark-colored, American-vehicle that looked like a Ford Crown Victoria, but Williams didn't get very far. Apparently, the bullet hit a major artery and he bled to death. His body was found by the police a few minutes later after his accomplice pushed him out of the car on a West Oakland street.

S tabbing yourself is another painful way to end a crime. That's what happened when a man stole about three hundred dollars worth of hunting knives from a Meijer, Inc. superstore in Grand Rapids, Michigan, and hid them in the waistband of his pants so no one would see them. When he tried to leave the store, though, he was confronted by some employees, and after a short scuffle, he fled the store. He might have made a clean getaway, but he tripped, and was stabbed in the abdomen by one of the hunting knives still in his pants. Emergency personnel took him the hospital, while the police began their investigation.

Another extremely painful way to end a crime is to set yourself on fire. A thief in Atlanta, Georgia, broke into a convenience store to steal scratch-off lottery tickets. Before he left, he tried to destroy the evidence by setting the store on fire. He sprayed the store with charcoal lighter fluid, but waited to finish his crime before he struck a match. Unfortunately, by that time, the fumes from the lighter fluid had accumulated in the air, and instead of merely setting the store on fire, he also managed to light himself on fire.

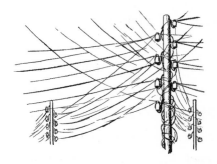

An even more painful way to end your crime is to electrocute yourself. In Dallas, Texas, a man climbed up a utility pole to try to steal copper from the wires. Unfortunately for him, when he tried to strip the wires, he received two shocks of over seven thousand volts. He lived, but suffered from third-degree burns over half of his body.

At least the rest of these stupid criminals lived. One robber from Fresno, California, wasn't so lucky. The thief used a screwdriver to rob a Mexican restaurant in the middle of the night, and then escaped on a bicycle with the money he had managed to steal. Minutes later, though, the police found the man. He had apparently crashed his bike and accidently impaled himself on his screwdriver. The screwdriver severed an artery in his leg, and he quickly bled to death.

ABOUT THE AUTHOR

Gini Graham Scott, PhD, JD., is a nationally known writer, consultant, speaker, and seminar leader. Originally from New York, Dr. Scott lives in both Santa Monica and Oakland, California. She has published over fifty books on diverse subjects, including humor and criminal justice, among them *Homicide by the Rich and Famous* and *American Murder*. Her PhD in Sociology is from the University of California, Berkeley, and her JD is from the University of San Francisco Law School.